—THE

ART OF WAITING

Text copyright © Wendy Bray 2004
The author asserts the moral right
to be identified as the author of this work

Published by
The Bible Reading Fellowship
First Floor, Elsfield Hall
15–17 Elsfield Way, Oxford OX2 8FG
ISBN 1 84101 296 3
First published 2004
10 9 8 7 6 5 4 3 2 1 0
All rights reserved

Acknowledgments
Unless otherwise stated, scripture quotations are taken from the Holy
Bible, New International Version, copyright © 1973, 1978, 1984 by
International Bible Society, are used by permission of Hodder &
Stoughton Limited. All rights reserved. 'NIV' is a registered trademark of
International Bible Society. UK trademark number 1448790.

Extracts from the Authorized Version of the Bible (The King James Bible),
the rights in which are vested in the Crown, are reproduced by
permission of the Crown's patentee, Cambridge University Press.

THE MESSAGE copyright © by Eugene H. Peterson 1993, 1994, 1995.
Used by permission of NavPress Publishing Group.

Christmas Day prayer copyright © Wendy Bray/Care for the Family 2001.
'Lord, I come to you' by Geoff Bullock, copyright © 1992 Word Music
Inc. / Maranatha! Music. Used by permission.

A catalogue record for this book is available from the British Library

Printed and bound in Great Britain by
Bookmarque, Croydon

—THE—
ART OF WAITING

WENDY BRAY

Daily Reflections for the Advent season

acknowledgments

Thank you to those who have shared their unique 'waiting' stories with me for this book: Hayley (and Oscar), Debra, Dawn, David and Chris—and, as ever, to Naomi, Eithne and the team at BRF for their help and support.

A special thank you to my lovely and long-suffering husband Richard, who puts up with having his life spread out on the pages of my writing all too often, and Lois and Benjamin, who 'don't mind too much'. 'Love you!'

CONTENTS

INTRODUCTION

How to use *The Art of Waiting*

Whenever I know I'll have to spend some time waiting, I get prepared! Whether I'll be waiting for a train, in the waiting-room at the hospital for the regular post-cancer check-ups I need, or outside my son's school while he finishes a basketball game, I'll take along with me at least a book, probably some writing, and very often a personal CD player.

To make the most of *The Art of Waiting* you could follow the same philosophy. As you wait on God with each daily reading, take along a 'waiting kit' including a Bible, a notebook and pen to write down your thoughts, and perhaps some music.

Art is expressed in a wide variety of ways that often complement each other—poetry with music, or words with illustration. Ask God to speak to you through any means you use to listen to him 'while you wait'.

How to develop *The Art of Waiting*

Each week of readings begins with a wander into an imaginary gallery to view a work of art—perhaps a painting or sculpture. The first painting gives an introduction not just to the theme of the book but also to some of the subjects who appear in later works in the gallery. All the characters or subjects are drawn together in the final piece, and every one is, in some way, waiting.

This private view will literally set the scene for the week ahead, helping you to draw out the detail in the Bible readings that follow and to reflect on what God might be saying to you day by day. Five days of Bible readings are followed by a simple one-line personal reflection. You may then be invited to pray, write a few words or act practically on what you have read. Two special readings each week, usually at the weekend, are designed to approach the theme somewhat differently. They include the personal story of someone who knows what it is to wait, and a reflection or meditation that draws together the threads of the week's theme.

Journalling *The Art of Waiting*

I've already mentioned using a notebook to record your thoughts and prayers. If you are used to journal- or diary-keeping, this will be a familiar activity. If it isn't, why not try it? Journal keeping can be a marvellous way of keeping track of our own spiritual journey, enabling us to look back at the way God has spoken into our everyday lives.

There is no right or wrong way to keep a journal. Simply record what you have read, your own thoughts, perhaps one or two pointers for prayer, maybe a practical application and, most importantly, what you think God might be saying to you. It may be just one or two words, a point of teaching or a clear impression of something that links your reading with a situation you are facing.

Write in a way that seems most natural to you, perhaps as if you are writing to a friend who knows you well. Be creative. If you can draw (or even if you think you can't) consider drawing your thoughts too. A detailed illustration or a watery sketch, a strong symbol or a rambling doodle can all reflect our hearts and thoughts in response to God and his word.

Your journal is for your eyes only, and for God's ears. You can pour out your heart on its pages or just jot a few words on a line. However or whatever you write, draw, hear or say, give your words and actions to God as part of your time with him, and ask him to speak to you through them, as you wait.

Although *The Art of Waiting* is written as an Advent book, its themes are not exclusive to the Advent season. We wait at all times and in all circumstances. It is my prayer that its words will be relevant and practical whenever and wherever waiting is required!

Why learn the art of waiting?

David Stewart-David, an academic,[1] spent four years, thousands of pounds and 92 days standing in 2000 queues conducting interviews, before mentioning that his research had done nothing to make him more patient and concluding that 'no one likes waiting a long time!'

There is definitely an art to waiting, but unlike the 3D vision of the sculptor, the watercolour artist's lightness of touch or the natural rhythm of a concert pianist, the skills required to wait well can be learnt by us all. We can learn through experience, through patience, and by studying the art of those who have become, or are on the way to becoming, masters.

Almost every part of our daily lives involves a mix of waiting, planning and anticipation—from the simplicity of waiting for a kettle to boil or a bus to arrive, to the emotion wrapped around the wait for a much-loved friend to step on to the platform from a cross-country train or for a phone call that might bring the news we dread. Waiting can be an impatient stomp, a clockwards glance or a long and painful yearning. It almost always involves looking forward to what might be, perhaps a fear of the unknown and occasionally a foretaste of disappointment. But however and whyever we wait, it's a whole lot easier if we know what or whom we're waiting for and how long the wait will be.

What's difficult about waiting is that we're never quite sure whether we need to park our expectations in the short-stay or long-stay spaces, and we spend a lot of time with the nagging suspicion that if we opt for the short-stay, we're very likely to have an excess ticket slapped painfully on the windscreen of our life. It's the loss of control we find difficult, the unknown quantity. We feel vulnerable. We are at the mercy not just of the wait itself, but also of what or who controls it. Even if we have the patience of Job and (in Britain, at any rate) a national reputation for queuing, it's still difficult to wait if we ultimately feel we cannot trust the one who has the power to blow the whistle on our waiting game.

Each of us who lives the Christian life in the best way we can is being asked to wait, however, and to wait for things as yet unseen, in faith, trust and hope. We have no difficulty choosing the ticket this time. We know it's a long-term choice.

As we embark on the waiting period that is the Advent season, stretching to Christmas and a few days beyond, we'll discover why we're asked to wait, what we should be doing while we wait, and ultimately what we are waiting for, and we'll begin to see how God uses our everyday waiting times to parallel the journey that is our spiritual life. Through those times he teaches us patience, encourages us to trust him and his plan, and urges us to fix our eyes on his Son as our master and guide. He also gives us some insight into what we are ultimately waiting for—the crowning joy of our salvation, the salvation that heralds our longed-for relationship with him as he intended—the only joy that really is worth waiting for. It is salvation that the New Testament assures us of.

But now he has appeared once for all at the end of the ages to do away with sin by the sacrifice of himself. Just as man is destined to die once, and after that to face judgment, so Christ was sacrificed once to take away the sins of many people; and he will appear a second time, not to bear sin, but to bring salvation to those who are waiting for him.
HEBREWS 9:26b–28

USING 'THE ART OF WAITING' WITH SMALL GROUPS

Small groups could use *The Art of Waiting* as part of a series of Advent reflections. Each week has its own theme from which three main areas of focus are developed:

- *Waiting breathlessly:* Our wait with creation for God's plan to be ultimately fulfilled.
- *Active waiting:* Our wait for God to fulfil his plan in our individual lives.
- *A father in waiting:* God's wait for us as 'daily prodigals'.

Weekly themes are as follows:

Week 1: *Learning skills from the masters (1–7 December):* Exploring how some of the key characters in the Bible faced waiting times, and how those waiting times were woven into God's plan.

Week 2: *How to trust without holding your breath (8–14 December):* Trusting and worrying—including how we do the first and why we should stop doing the second.

Week 3: *Don't just sit there! Do something! (15–21 December):* The practicalities of waiting—what we do as we wait, where our focus should be and what our attitude should become.

Week 4: *Patience becomes hope (22–28 December):* How patience and hope walk hand in hand through any waiting time—a consideration of some Christmas themes surrounding waiting.

Week 5: *Hoping in things unseen (29 December–4 January):* Waiting in vain, in darkness and in difficult times. Embracing hope when all else is lost.

Week 6: *When the waiting is over (5–6 January):* What it is that we are *really* waiting for—gaining an eternal perspective.

Ways of using *The Art of Waiting*

It would be helpful if each group member used a copy of *The Art of Waiting* for daily personal reading. The group could then gather together weekly to read, pray and reflect on the week's theme.

At each session, begin by reading the week's introduction and then use one of the following three suggestions.

1) Use the two weekend readings (omitted or repeated as part of personal daily readings) as the basis for the session, dividing the evening into two parts as follows.

Part 1: Read the personal story together, sharing ideas and making connections with the life experiences of group members. Try to draw out some of the specific ways in which the 'story' illustrates both God's wait for us and our wait for the fulfilment of God's purpose in our lives.

Use readings and reflections from other days of the week to underline the weekly theme (faith, hope, and so on). Encourage the group members to apply these observations to their own lives.

Break for refreshment.

Part 2: Use the second weekend reading as a basis for a quieter time of reflection or meditation, as appropriate for your group. You might like to indicate the change of mood by lighting a candle, playing a short piece of music as an introduction, or sharing an opening prayer as you begin.

Ask God to help each of you to focus on him, and consider how he might be speaking both to the group and into individual lives, through your reading and reflection.

Close the session with the final prayer.

2) Spend some time before the session reflecting on your own response to the readings as group facilitator. Consider how these might dovetail with the responses of others. In a more informal

discussion, ask for contributions and thoughts from group members, drawn from the daily readings covered so far that week.

Again, try to draw out one or two key points for practical application. Close with one of the daily prayers or reflections.

3) Prepare your own reflection or study based on one or more of the Bible passages and readings included in a weekly theme.

A choice of prayers, reflections and personal stories could also be used as part of a Sunday service throughout the weeks of Advent, with each theme forming the basis of a sermon or short talk.

✣

LEARNING SKILLS
FROM THE MASTERS

GALLERY: 'THE CROWD IN WAITING'

Before you is a wide, expansive canvas, the first of a pair. You have glimpsed its twin in the distance, further along the gallery. But for now your breath is taken away by the magnificence of this first painting, and most specifically by its glorious riot of colour, shape and texture.

That colour, rich and intense at the bottom, lightens to a brilliant dizzying golden glow at the very top, drawing your eye ever upwards. You wonder at the imagination and creativity behind this tapestry of hue, this glorious, jewelled embroidery of light and tone, depth and surface, shadow and light, boldness and fragility. The colour may be rich, even eccentric, but the paint has been skilfully applied in painstaking detail.

You step back in an attempt to take in not just the size and scope of the painting, but also the figures portrayed, for it shows you a crowd of humanity. Men and women, children and babies, old and young are assembled here before you. Some stand alone; others walk together, hands linked or arms entwined. A few rely on the support of those around them: a sighted man stands with one blinded, his head bowed, as if describing the sights. The strong carry the weak. Those in pain, and there are many, are grey-faced and often alone.

There are people from all walks of life, all ages of time, all professions, all trades, all nations. There is a medieval farmer with his plough, a black jazz musician apparently soulfully struggling to make his instrument heard, an office worker with an overflowing in-tray. Children are chasing here and there, round and between the legs of parents. Babies reach out for their mothers, young women blush at the sight of young men. A footballer celebrates the scoring of a goal with an upward leap, his fist punching the air. A cook tastes a spoonful of the ingredients he is preparing in a large mixing bowl, while an opera singer curtsies to receive a flamboyant bouquet. To one side, shunned by most of the passing crowd, a beggar holds out his hand in supplication, his clothes torn and muddied, an ugly scar across his forehead.

A clergyman is marrying a blushing bride and a nervously hunched groom. Two men are building a wall, one bending for the mortar, the other lifting a pile of new bricks. A woman stands weeping, her hands pressed to her tear-stained cheeks, alone, even in such a crowd. Youths wander apparently aimlessly, with scowls on their faces and their hands deep in their pockets. Two businessmen are shaking on a deal, bulging briefcases at their feet.

You see aggression and tenderness, intention and regret, work and play all portrayed here. You cannot imagine how many weeks and months the painter took to achieve such detail. What vision kept him at his canvas through day and night? It is as if he knows each one portrayed, wonderfully capturing the fears and frustrations, needs, joys and hidden gifts of each personality. The dreams they dream, the plans they have made, the hope and disappointment they carry, have somehow been made visible.

You look again to see a woman. A shawl is pulled around her shoulders, a tiny child is held close and she is looking into the far distance, anxiety furrowing her brow. Beyond her gaze, two trapeze artists swing from a highwire above, frozen in mid-air and in time. On a high shelf to one side, a beautiful clock sits in full view of the crowd. A few faces are lifted towards it, expectant, as if waiting for it to chime or to watch its hands move into place.

This is the busyness, the bustle, the beautiful ordinariness and tragic tenderness that is life. But there is a paradox in this painting. Despite the hectic pace of life portrayed, the hum of activity, the purpose and intention, the 'going everywhere fast' that is set before you, there is a sense of going nowhere slowly—of being stuck on the down escalator of life when you were expecting to go up.

Looking closer, you notice that in the midst of it all there is a sense of frustrated expectancy, a 'not yet' on the breeze, a call for patience. There is a hesitancy that you can't quite place despite the boldness of the brushwork.

Then you begin to understand the artist's intention. This is a waiting crowd—waiting not for something to be shared or for a play to start, but for a word, a word that will set them free from the frenetic pace they have set themselves, a word that will dry their tears, ease their pain and restore their sight. A word that will tell them that they can indeed pass beyond this place, that their wait is over, that it is 'time'.

And then you locate the hidden essence of that word in a face or two. It is etched into the weary lines, the tired eyes. It is hope.

Hope is reflected in the faces of those who are turned towards the light that is spread across the sky above and ahead of them. Those who are apparently leading the crowd are turned away from the bustle of activity and fixing their gaze on the golden light above. It appears to have revived those whose energy is almost gone; it has given a sense of urgency to those whose work is not quite finished and begun to illustrate the first of a million answers to those who just can't stop asking questions.

As you reluctantly walk away from the painting, you wonder how many more will lift their faces, and how long they have to wait. And more than anything, you sense from that portrayal of hope that this is not the end of their story. Something of the hope reflected on those upturned faces reassures you that whatever it is they are waiting for, it will be worth it.

INTRODUCTION

As Christians we know that we're ultimately waiting for God to fulfil his wonderful plan of salvation. During the Advent season we have an opportunity to focus and reflect on that wait.

So, if we know what and whom it is we're waiting for, shouldn't our wait be a whole lot easier? Shouldn't we at least be able to develop some elementary waiting skills? The problem is, we can't be sure how long our wait will be and, in our impatient human state, we find that tough. We may even occasionally wonder if God has 'lost the plot', is facing 'unavoidable delays', or if he has forgotten us altogether.

Part of an artist's training involves studying the masters, the great artists of past years, looking at their technique, their skills, their unique style, and trying to catch their vision. This is not so that the students can simply copy what they see, but so that they can understand the creative process. In this first week of Advent, we're going to look at the work of a few 'waiting' artists. We'll consider the techniques they used as they patiently waited for God, what helped them wait, and how a glimpse of their lives might help us as we develop our own approach to waiting. We can imagine that the metaphorical 'artwork' that their waiting lives produced is displayed in our gallery.

While they may have elements and skills in common, each illustration of waiting is unique, dependent on the experience, vision and technique of the individual 'artist'. For example, the apostle Paul's painting is bold and authoritative. He uses oils for permanence and his colours are vibrant, while his brush strokes are confident and uncompromising. He knows the message he wants to send and he fills every area of his canvas in the process. His detail directs our eyes heavenwards, offering a sure and certain hope.

Abraham's has been more slowly executed; he has laboured over the composition and has taken his time. Occasionally he has even messed up. Yet his art has a permanence and sense of faithfulness that draws us in and sets the tone for the artists that follow him.

Mary's is a delicate watercolour, patiently composed. She has followed her master's instructions to the brush stroke. It is bravely executed, with complex detail and breathtaking perspective that she cannot have envisioned when she began, but which reached triumphant completion as she mixed colours and shades like wine and water, tears and blood.

Joseph's piece, understandably, is a carving. He has allowed the colour and knots of the wood free rein to express their life and age, and to tell their own story. The carving resembles a simple cradle from one angle, but from the other it throws a shadow on the white walls of the gallery—the shadow of a cross.

A line of unfinished canvasses stretches beyond these key works. These are paintings not yet hung. They are waiting to be completed and will take their place in the gallery when the time is right. Some have just a few pencil strokes trailing across their surface or are waiting for more colour and detail to be added. Others are almost finished, needing just a few finishing touches.

These are *our* pieces of art, awaiting completion. They are 'work in progress'.

PAUL AND A LONGED-FOR BIRTH

The creation waits in eager expectation for the sons of God to be revealed. For the creation was subjected to frustration, not by its own choice, but by the will of the one who subjected it, in hope that the creation itself will be liberated from its bondage to decay and brought into the glorious freedom of the children of God. We know that the whole creation has been groaning as in the pains of childbirth right up to the present time. Not only so, but we ourselves, who have the firstfruits of the spirit, groan inwardly as we wait eagerly for our adoption as sons, the redemption of our bodies. For in this hope we were saved. But hope that is seen is no hope at all. Who hopes for what he already has? But if we hope for what we do not yet have, we wait for it patiently.

ROMANS 8:19–25

These verses really are a song of Advent waiting. They are the ongoing anthem of creation and the ballad of salvation rolled into one, with the yearning of a love song.

Creation is waiting, Paul explains, because God has put the brakes on, held it up, made it wait—but for a glorious purpose. It is his plan that instead of sinking into bondage and decay, creation can be liberated.

God the creator just loves his creation. (Remember, in Genesis 1:31, 'God saw all that he had made, and it was very good'.) He wants to see it restored in all its glory, in a glorious, all-encompassing relationship with him—new heavens and a new earth. First and foremost, that includes our relationship with him as father, so Paul uses a very human illustration to make his point.

It may seem strange for Paul, not known for his feminine sympathies, to portray creation in waiting in such a maternal way. Even Paul must have known that when he was speaking of a new life longed for and laboured for, he could hardly escape the birth illustration. There is something familiar, yet exciting in the way that such a commonplace—but none the less miraculous—event as the birth of a child is used to assure us of the even more exciting eventuality God has planned for us. Even those who do not or cannot know the experience of expecting a child or the enjoyment of a relationship with a parent can know this hope as God-given. We do not need to have previously experienced family life to enjoy a perfect relationship with our Father God—the most natural and fulfilling relationship of all.

A friend of mine, a counsellor and social worker who often leads seminars on family and adoption issues, tells the wonderful story of waiting for his first child. He and his wife had been hoping for a baby for some years, but after numerous medical tests and consultations it became apparent that they would not be able to have a child of their own.

After much heart-searching, they decided to apply for adoption, hoping to give their love and care to a baby who could become their own. They had never-ending paperwork to complete, difficult and stressful interviews and assessments to face, and a long and agonizing wait. It often seemed that they would never have the child they longed for. Then they were asked to visit a baby boy in foster care with a view to adoption. It was love at first sight, at least for my friend's wife—my friend took a little longer! But through, or despite, the nappies and wet kisses, this needy little boy reached my friend's heart.

They returned home full of hope, but within a few days complications arose that cast doubt over whether this baby could be the one to start their family. Another anxious wait followed, many tears, and some desperation. Then one morning my friend received a telephone call in the middle of a seminar. It was his wife. She had heard from the adoption agency: the little boy could be theirs.

My friend says he remembers that day as if it was yesterday, despite the fact that his 'little boy' has just left university. There are many times when he looks at his tall, energetic son and remembers the wait for him, the call that made it all worthwhile, and the moment when he officially became a dad. He had waited patiently for a relationship he had only ever been able to long for. The small baby who became a strapping son is a constant reminder of hope fulfilled.

How does it feel to wait and hope for 'what is unseen' (2 Corinthians 4:18)? It is something like the deep yearning that envelops us when we long for a child, the ache of longing that joins two lovers who are far apart and the homesickness for hills and fields when we are confined to city streets. Through such experiences, God can plant a seed in our hearts that grows into a longing for him, a hope of relationship with him, and a hope for all he has prepared for us. It's just that often we don't recognize it as such, and live believing that it is the things 'seen' that will fill the gap, ease the longing, meet the need. They don't, of course. Our greatest need is for God.

Our greatest hope is for the unseen that God has promised us— our eternal life with the one who loves us more than we can ever imagine. For that, as Paul says, we must wait patiently. And expect some groaning along the way!

Reflect...

What am I really waiting for?

Father, patience is not my virtue; waiting is not my favourite game. But a plan like yours needs time to reach perfection, time to touch hearts, time to reach the lost. As I wait for what I do not have, give me hope.

ABRAHAM: THE PROFESSIONAL WAITER

Consider Abraham: 'He believed God, and it was credited to him as righteousness.' Understand, then, that those who believe are children of Abraham. The Scripture foresaw that God would justify the Gentiles by faith, and announced the gospel in advance to Abraham: 'All nations will be blessed through you.' So those who have faith are blessed along with Abraham, the man of faith.

GALATIANS 3:6–9

Abraham was a professional waiter. I don't mean that he was an expert with a folded tea towel and silver service—well, not as far as we know! What I mean is that he was so used to periods of waiting throughout his life that he must have become something of an expert. His neighbours may even have given him a nickname. ('Hang-around-ham', maybe?)

One simple phrase sums up old Ham's attitude to waiting: 'Abraham believed God'. When God said something to Abraham, Abraham simply believed him. He didn't close one eye suspiciously and mutter 'I wonder…' under his breath, or suggest that pigs might take off nearby at any moment. He just believed him. He had faith.

I wonder if God chose to make an amusing illustration out of Abraham's faith just to ease the strain of waiting? God told him, when he was over 60, that Sarah his wife would have a son and that the birth would make him the 'father of all nations'. The thought was hilarious to both husband and wife. In those days before the trend for older mothers, Sarah was, understandably, somewhat dubious. Abraham, once he had stopped chuckling, 'believed God' (see Genesis 17:17—18:12). He had to face a bit of a wait, but when Abraham was 100 years old, Isaac was born to Sarah—and she literally had the last laugh (Genesis 21:6–7) of joy!

Imagine the irony of the birth announcement card: 'To Sarah and Abraham—After a long wait, a son, Isaac.' After all, most of us find nine months quite long enough, but Abraham waited decades for God's unbelievable promise to be fulfilled. I bet he boasted just a bit about that 'father' title. Well, wouldn't you?

Abraham died at the age of 175, a 'man of faith' (Galatians 3:9), still 'believing God' for the 'great nation' he had been promised (Genesis 12:2). As he had waited, he had trusted God. He was obedient. He was patient. He held on to an eternal hope.

My teenage son loves Christmas cake. In fact, he loves Christmas cake so much that he has started requesting it as his birthday cake in the summer too! Having watched and helped over the years, he knows that making the Christmas cake involves a long, slow process using top-quality ingredients, begun, by family tradition, in the autumn half-term week.

He starts getting excited just watching those ingredients appear in the larder. I buy them gradually—the sultanas and raisins one week, the cherries and dried apricots the next (no one likes candied peel in our house), then the nuts and sugar. Then, when the time comes, he'll help me mix it, guard it during its time in the oven, watch it cool and, once it is wrapped, remind me periodically to 'brandy the cake'. Then he loves watching (and sniffing!) as I take the brown paper parcel containing the cake out of the cupboard, unwrap it and then, pricking it with a skewer, drizzle brandy across the surface of the cake until it sinks down into the fruity depths.

I dare not buy the marzipan until it's time for the cake to be covered (marzipan is something we all like too much). We all help decide how I'll decorate the top. Suggestions range from the ridiculous to the traditional. We've had perky-looking penguins, whole nativity scenes and peaceful snowy doves (although not all at the same time), but I always try to make sure that everyone has at least been consulted, as this is very much a family cake.

So after all the hard work, one of my little Christmas Day joys, and one of Benjamin's rather larger ones, is watching him eat his first slice. He'll cut it, spend a few moments looking at it, sniff the fruit, nibble a tiny piece of marzipan and icing, then take the first bite, his face dissolving into a blissful smile as he finishes it. 'Perfect,' he says. 'Worth the wait.'

Trust, obedience, patience and hope: they are the ingredients of faith used in the art of good waiting for Abraham, and for my son. They can help us as we wait, both in our everyday lives and in our longer wait for the fulfilment of God's plan—a plan that is perfect, and worth the wait countless times over.

Reflect...

What is the one thing I always feel is really worth waiting for?

Father, you know every detail of your plan. Each tiny part bears your name. It points to your will for me, speaks of your love for me. Help me trust you as it unfolds, obey you as I play my part, have patience when the wait is long, look forward to that eternal hope.

MARY AND THE BABY THAT WOULD SAVE THE WORLD

And Mary said:

> 'My soul glorifies the Lord
> and my spirit rejoices in God my saviour,
> for he has been mindful
> of the humble state of his servant.
> From now on all generations will call me blessed,
> for the Mighty One has done great things for me—
> holy is his name.
> His mercy extends to those who fear him,
> from generation to generation.
> He has performed mighty deeds with his arm;
> he has scattered those who are proud in their inmost thoughts.
> He has brought down rulers from their thrones
> but has lifted up the humble.
> He has filled the hungry with good things
> but has sent the rich away empty.
> He has helped his servant Israel,
> remembering to be merciful
> to Abraham and his descendants forever,
> even as he said to our fathers.'

Mary stayed with Elizabeth for about three months and then returned home.

LUKE 1:46–56

I can remember, as if it were yesterday, the day my first pregnancy was confirmed. A home test kit had almost confirmed our suspicions on Mothering Sunday (God's wonderful sense of humour). A lab test the following day agreed (something as important as new life needs a double safeguard) and I was officially an expectant mum.

I probably should have exercised a little caution and kept 'mum' about it for a few weeks, but such was my excitement that I wanted to tell everyone. I can remember hurrying down the hill into town to do some shopping, because of course I had no time to lose in looking for baby gear—there were only nine months, after all! I was almost bursting with excitement. I contemplated sharing my news with a traffic warden I passed, two elderly men drinking cider on a bench, and a window cleaner. None looked as if they would be too impressed. In the end I could bear it no longer and told the assistant in the first babywear shop I came to. She graciously didn't disclose the probability that dozens of new mums rushed in to do the same thing each week.

Thinking of that experience, I enjoy this picture of Mary rushing off to share her amazing news with her cousin Elizabeth, who had waited long and patiently for her own special pregnancy. No shortcut of email or phone call for Mary. This visit involved quite a journey—but oh, the excitement once they got together! We couldn't have blamed Mary and Elizabeth if all they wanted to do was spend the day comparing swaddling cloth patterns or baskets for the babies to sleep in. But notice what Mary does first: her heart is turned to God in a prophetic song of delight and praise.

The last verse in our reading reassures us, though, that Mary and Elizabeth were real, flesh-and-blood women. Mary stayed with Elizabeth for about three months—enough time to help her prepare for her baby, for the two of them to dream and plan together and, I suspect, laugh and chatter quite a lot too. I like to think that during that stay, Zechariah, Elizabeth's husband, sent his eyebrows heavenward and sought refuge among the other men in the village occasionally.

Then Mary returned home to prepare for what, and whom, she was waiting for. Yet she must have suspected that she knew only half of it. God had yet to reveal the full extent and wonder of his plan and the part Mary would continue to play. She was waiting not just for a child but also for her whole life's purpose to unfold as she became part of the fulfilment of God's eternal plan. In simple faith, these women from ordinary backgrounds played more significant roles than they could have dreamed in the love story involving all of us who call that tiny baby, born to one of them, Lord.

I love the soft and intricate figure drawings of Italian artists such as Leonardo da Vinci and Michelangelo, which provided the outline for their great painted masterpieces. They have a depth and sensitivity that few artists have managed to capture since. I would love to have been able to watch them work as curves became limbs and small details gave smiles to lips, light to eyes and glow to faces.

One of my favourites is in the National Gallery in London. It is a detail from Leonardo's *The Virgin and Child with Saint Anne and Saint John the Baptist*. It is only a charcoal and chalk drawing on tinted paper, but it is beautiful. Mary's face is gentle, full of quiet joy at what God has done, yet at the same time it carries the watchfulness and contentment of mothers the world over.

When I was a child I often played a 'Step by step' drawing game with my dad. He would draw just a few marks on a blank page, then a few more, until a picture was complete. I would try hard to guess what he was creating with each line and shape, but would rarely recognize the full picture until the last pencil stroke was drawn. God's way is often similar. He can be almost tantalizing in the way he asks us to wait for the full picture to be revealed. We may not understand the meaning of all he is drawing around us until the day he stands beside us with our life rolled out like a precious canvas before our eyes. Then we will understand at last the curves, lines and detail that he has drawn over the years of the life that is uniquely ours.

Reflect...

Is there a line or curve in the drawing of my life that I cannot understand?

Creator God, help me trust your design for each line, curve and detail of my life. I can have no idea how your plan for me might become part of your plan for humankind. But you are the most skilled of artists and will paint a masterpiece.

JOSEPH AND THE BABY
THAT BEAT THE ODDS

This is how the birth of Jesus came about: His mother Mary was pledged to be married to Joseph, but before they came together, she was found to be with child through the Holy Spirit. Because Joseph her husband was a righteous man and did not want to expose her to public disgrace, he had in mind to divorce her quietly. But after he had considered this, an angel of the Lord appeared to him in a dream and said, 'Joseph son of David, do not be afraid to take Mary home as your wife, because what is conceived in her is from the Holy Spirit. She will give birth to a son, and you are to give him the name Jesus, because he will save his people from their sins.'

All this took place to fulfil what the Lord had said through the prophet: 'The virgin will be with child and will give birth to a son, and they will call him Immanuel'—which means, 'God with us.' When Joseph woke up, he did what the angel of the Lord commanded him and took Mary home as his wife. But he had no union with her until she gave birth to a son, and he gave him the name Jesus.

MATTHEW 1:18–25

It can be hard to find ways to read the story of the birth of Jesus in a fresh way. Sometimes, as Christmas approaches, I try to maintain a focus on the story from the perspective of one particular personality—the innkeeper perhaps, or Joseph.

We hear little about Joseph the carpenter, or what he must have felt, only that he did as God asked. The Gospel story bears witness to his faithfulness, both to Mary as a husband and to Jesus as an earthly father. Perhaps Joseph was the strong, silent type—just what the teenager Mary needed in the bewildering months surrounding Jesus' birth and over the years that followed. We can only imagine him teaching the young Jesus to trace a grain in a piece of wood and use a plane and lathe, or reminding him to sweep the wood shavings from the floor and to check his measurements for accuracy before making the first cut. Was he aware of the privilege of teaching the Son of God? All we can be certain of is that Joseph was chosen, like Mary, to play a vital part in God's unfolding family saga.

Sometimes we hear stories of how members of succeeding generations of one family have become Christians, often as a result of the faithful and devoted prayer of grandparents. When I was at college, one of my friends told me how her grandmother, Jean, kept a childhood promise made in the 1920s to pray for her school-friend, Vivienne. Vivienne's family didn't attend the little mission hall in the village where Jean and Vivienne lived as children and, as this bothered young Jean somewhat, she promised a bewildered but grateful Vivienne that she would pray for her—always.

Vivienne and Jean lost touch just before the war, but Jean kept her word and never stopped praying for her friend. She also prayed for her granddaughter, my friend Sue, right through Sue's difficult teenage years. Sue eventually became a Christian, much to Jean's delight, and it was then that Jean told her about her lifelong prayers for friends and family, including Vivienne, and her hope that God would show her how her prayers had been answered.

Sue met Simon at a Christian Union training day. They got to know one another, fell in love, and decided to get married. Inevitably Sue was invited up to Scotland to meet Simon's large extended family, and went off feeling somewhat nervous but intrigued, having heard that every adult in the 18-strong family was a Christian. Sue was warmly welcomed and enjoyed a wonderful weekend, but that wasn't what brought her running into my college room on her return. During the course of the weekend Sue had met Simon's grandmother—and yes, you've guessed it, Simon's grandmother was Vivienne. She had come to faith many years before and, remembering Jean's promise and prayer, was sad that they had lost touch. Through a series of questions about Sue's family, first to Simon, she had begun to put two and two together. When Sue agreed that this particular two and two did make four, Vivienne wept with joy.

On hearing the story, Jean simply smiled, closed her eyes momentarily and whispered the words, 'At last. Thank you.' Her waiting had been rewarded. Needless to say, the two grandmothers had quite a lot to say to each other at the wedding!

In another series of connections, I remember the joy of discovering as a teenager that I could trace the foretelling of the coming of Christ from the Old Testament to the New. I marvelled at the way God's waiting plan involved so many individual lives fitting perfectly together in obedience and faith (see Isaiah 7:14). I became very excited about the way so many Old Testament prophecies had been fulfilled in the New. I jotted down a few notes at the time, but heard the details again, very recently, in a sermon.

I'm not into numbers, being a word girl myself, but these facts and figures impressed even me. In *Evidence that Demands a Verdict*,[2] Josh McDowell includes a quote from Professor Peter Stoner, who took just eight of sixty major prophecies relating the coming of Christ and applied the science of probability: 'We find that the chance that any man might have lived down to the present time and fulfilled all eight prophecies is 1 in 10 to the power of 17 (i.e. 1 in 100,000,000,000,000,000).' For those of us who would rather think in words and pictures, Stoner illustrates this by suggesting that if we took the same number of silver dollars, they would cover the state of Texas two feet deep. We could then mark one coin in that huge sea of silver and ask one man to travel where he wants over that sea and make just one selection. The chances, Stoner said, that he will pick up the right coin first time are the same as the chance of all eight prophecies coming true in one man—Jesus. Consider, then, the staggering odds against all 60 major prophecies being fulfilled in him.

That, in words and numbers, is the 'loving against the odds' love story of God that Joseph, you and I, and millions of others like Jean, Sue and Vivienne, are part of.

Reflect...

Take time to stand amazed at your small part in God's perfect plan.

Father God, I realize that from generation to generation your plan is slowly being unfolded and fulfilled. All creation really does wait expectantly, as so many before me have waited in assurance of your 'against the odds' love. Thank you that I am one of that multitude.

RESULTS THAT CHART NEW WATERS

For you created my inmost being;
you knit me together in my mother's womb.
I praise you because I am fearfully and wonderfully made;
your works are wonderful,
I know that full well.
My frame was not hidden from you
when I was made in the secret place.
When I was woven together in the depths of the earth,
your eyes saw my unformed body.
All the days ordained for me
were written in your book
before one of them came to be.
How precious to me are your thoughts, O God!
How vast is the sum of them!
Were I to count them,
they would outnumber the grains of sand.
When I awake,
I am still with you.

PSALM 139:13–18

When I read through the life of David, especially his psalms, I always notice how much he talked to God. He spoke in everything from a desperate whisper to a cry of pain, in heated debate and with yells of frustration. David's words reveal how well he knew God, and how well God knew David—and nowhere more so than in this beautiful psalm.

David realized that nothing can be hidden from our all-knowing

God, and that God knew him even before he came to be. There was nothing about David, with all his flaws and gifts, that could be a surprise to God. He knew, and knows, everything that had happened, was happening and would happen to David, and to you and to me. What's more, he planned it.

Eugene Peterson paraphrases verses 15–16 in THE MESSAGE as: 'Like an open book, you watched me from conception to birth; all the stages of my life were spread out before you, the days of my life all prepared before I'd even lived one day.' I don't believe that those verses mean that God has designed us to live like marionettes, stiffly following a pre-prepared path, taking mechanical steps with no free will or creativity, no last-minute changes of plan or appeals to his heart. Instead, the stages of our lives help us plan a wonderful journey together with God—a journey with infinite possibilities and routes, like that shared between a wise and experienced sailor and his trainee. Together they navigate their voyage, watching the horizon, taking readings and getting results that will help chart the next leg.

I like to imagine God poring over that chart of our lives, listening to our heartfelt desires and watching our dreams as if they were illuminated on the horizon. He consults his great plan and draws out the infinite possibilities for mapping our dreams and desires together as part of that plan for the journey ahead. Our ultimate destination, our home port, is sure. It's only our individual route that varies. Sometimes he may decide on a definite way through because the geography or weather dictates it. At other times he can give us a bit more freedom to choose the route we want to chart. He may even allow us to get off course because a bit of time spent in choppy waters will have us looking to him as the great navigator again.

In that seagoing context, waiting can be like time spent in the doldrums—seemingly flat and endless days and nights when the wind is non-existent and, as a result, we seem to be going nowhere. We look heavenward and ask, 'Will we ever get going again?'

Few things have us looking heavenward from the doldrums quite like waiting for results or news—results of exams or medical tests, news of interviews or consultations, dreaded letters and e-mails—anything where our 'moving on' is dependent on the actions or decisions made by others, often on our behalf. Sometimes that news may be life-changing, with the power to move us on speedily, bring us to a standstill, or change our circumstances entirely. Yet, somehow, the waiting is the worst part.

Like so many, as a cancer patient I have known hours in hospital corridors, mentally watching my life parade before me because the results I am about to hear will tell me whether I can plan beyond just a few months ahead. I have busied myself while my children have paced the house waiting for the one man more elusive than Father Christmas—the postman—because he carries exam results or news of school places. The wait itself has seemed like an ever-inflating balloon that must either burst or carry us away in relief. It's as if nothing else in the world matters and, as we peer up the street in hope, we wonder how everyone else can carry on cleaning their windows or walking their dogs as normal.

If God really has spread out all the stages of our life before him, though, we can trust him to be in those results or between the lines of that news. He will have known what was contained in that brown envelope long before it was sealed. That doesn't mean he doesn't cry with us when the news is sad or, equally, rejoice with us when the results are good. He is with us, behind us and ahead of us, rooting for us, whatever.

Making prayerful choices beyond that good or bad news is the tough part. There may be some irony in the fact that we may need to wait on him as long after we have received what we've waited for as before. For here, on the paper clutched feverishly between our fingers or in the words still ringing in our ears, are God's compass bearings for the next part of our journey. We may not know where they will take us, but God does.

Reflect...

Think back to a time when significant news moved you on or changed the direction of your life. Can you now see God's hand on the tiller?

Father God, no matter how long I have waited, such significant moments are rarely 'the end' but the beginning of a new leg of our journey together. As I wait, give me your peace, filled with the knowledge that your charting is flawless, your compass bearings sure, 'for all the stages of my life are spread out before you'.

HAYLEY: A MUM IN WAITING

All around us we observe a pregnant creation. The difficult times of pain throughout the world are simply birth pangs. But it's not only around us; it's within us. The spirit of God is arousing us within. We're also feeling the birth pangs. These sterile and barren bodies of ours are yearning for full deliverance. That is why waiting does not diminish us, any more than waiting diminishes a pregnant mother. We are enlarged in the waiting. We, of course, don't see what is enlarging us. But the longer we wait, the larger we become, and the more joyful our expectancy.

ROMANS 8:19–25 (*The Message*)

Eugene Peterson's paraphrase of Paul's words from Romans draw an even more vivid picture of Paul's metaphorical teaching. They are certainly understood by mums in waiting.

Hayley Barnard lives in Plymouth with her husband Leigh and baby son Oscar, and was (albeit unknown to her) in the final week of her pregnancy when she shared her thoughts on waiting. Her experience illustrates something of what the apostle Paul meant about the expectation of the wonderful event that lies ahead for all of us who wait in faith. It also reminds us of just a few of the little frustrations of waiting, which miraculously disappear from memory immediately after a birth!

'One day, after a lot of thought, we said to each other, "Maybe we should start trying for a baby… we might have to wait ages to conceive." Famous last words! Three weeks later I found myself being very sick and visiting the loo a ridiculous amount of times day and night. Nine months of waiting stretched ahead of me. It seemed like an age. It felt like an age! As the weeks passed, however, there was, at last, visible proof that I was getting closer to the long-awaited event. My waistline rapidly disappeared and was replaced by a bump that has made me look more like an alien with each passing day.

'I have tried to enjoy the wait, using it to prepare myself as best I can, physically, but mainly mentally. Each stage has prepared me for the next and, to be honest, if I'd not had nine months to prepare, I can confidently say I would not have been in any fit state to handle labour or impending motherhood.

'One of the hardest things about the wait, particularly as I approach the end, is the constant stream of enquiries as to whether "the event" has happened. It is nice that people care and are interested but I wonder if these same people will be as interested when the baby is two months old and I am exhausted and struggling with piles of dirty nappies!

'A midwife friend of mine keeps trying to persuade me to tell everyone that my due date is two weeks later than it actually is, so as to ease the state of anticipation of those around me. But I can't. I've waited too long—my eyes are firmly fixed on the 26th of October.

'Having said this, I do wonder why my GP bothered to give me a specific date. After all, I've read that only six per cent of babies are born on the due date. This one is hardly likely to be one of the six per cent!

'Now that I am only days away from that "due date" I wonder if being given a "due window" of, say, three weeks, might have been easier to cope with—and certainly less disappointing should I still be waiting come Bonfire Night. I am hoping for something of a big explosion and accompanying celebration before then!

'I haven't prayed for patience until now—and now I'm almost too impatient to pray for patience. Until now, though, I have found the physical aspects of pregnancy quite bearable (yes, even the morning sickness). But now I would like the wait to be over. I'd like to be able to walk without a waddle. I'd like to be able to sleep on my tummy again. I'd like to be able to go for a few hours without visiting the loo. I'd like to be able to eat more than a few mouthfuls without feeling stuffed. Most of all, I'd like to meet the little person who has been kicking me for the past few months.

'I long for that special moment when my husband and I hold our first child in our arms. My mother always told me that good things come to those who wait. Well—I'm waiting!'

Ironically, unusually and in obliging style for the sake of this book (I must thank him one day!), baby Oscar beat the odds by becoming one of the six per cent: he arrived on his due date! In the end, Hayley didn't have to wait too much longer.

We don't know how long we will have to wait to see God face to face. But we do know that, like Hayley's and Leigh's wait for baby Oscar, our waiting and expectation will be over on exactly the due day. We may not be able to hurry that day, or name it, but we can look forward to it, maybe even long for it, especially when life becomes uncomfortable for us.

Meanwhile, there is much we can do to prepare ourselves for the ultimate fulfilment of what is already an amazing relationship. We can share our relationship with others, get to know the one we hope to meet through reading his word, and involve him fully in life in our waiting place through prayer. And we can look forward to meeting him—because we know that one day we will see him as he really is and stand before him as he always intended.

Reflect...

How 'expectant' am I? What can I do to prepare for the ultimate fulfilment of my relationship with God?

Father, the day will come when I will see you face to face. Give me a sense of expectancy and of excitement. Keep me looking heavenward as I wait, and remind me that I although I am not home yet, you are waiting for me.

PERSONAL PLANNING

'For I know the plans I have for you,' declares the Lord, 'plans to prosper you and not to harm you, plans to give you hope and a future. Then you will call upon me and come and pray to me, and I will listen to you. You will seek me and find me when you seek me with all your heart. I will be found by you,' declares the Lord, 'and will bring you back from captivity. I will gather you from all the nations and places where I have banished you,' declares the Lord, 'and will bring you back to the place from which I carried you into exile.'

JEREMIAH 29:11–14

These words were given to Jeremiah as he spoke to God's exiled people in Babylon. God laid out his plans for restoration before Jeremiah, and gave him the unenviable task of 'selling' them to the people. They were not easy to bear, involving, as they did, a 70-year wait not just for the restoration of their nation in its rightful place, but for restoration of a right relationship with God, a relationship as he had originally intended.

Despite the tenderness and hope in God's words in verses 12–14, many who heard those words knew that they would die in exile, long before the fulfilment of God's promises—even that their children and grandchildren would do the same. But God clearly reassured them that, despite the exile, he did have a future planned for them if they would repent and submit their lives to him—a prosperous and hopeful future.

I am fascinated by old architectural plans, especially of houses. I love the detail, the accuracy and the promise of something beautiful that grew from the vision of the architect who laboured over the drawings. I am always curious about the domestic life that filled those rooms, which have been transformed from mere lines of pencil-lead and purpose on a page to bricks and mortar, furnished reality, and the setting for family life. It's a transformation that is particularly intriguing if the architect knew the family for whom he was designing.

For similar reasons, I would love the opportunity to design and build my own home. I can sketch the idea roughly, draw up a list of the rooms I'd like and the materials I'd use, but that would be my limit. I can have a vision for my house but no way to realize it. I have no skills or experience to draw up the detailed plans and I do not understand the practicalities of plumbing or the realities and constraints of construction. I can see the finished dream in my head, but it is a nebulous, changeable one. At best, I can hold a flat and lifeless sketch of the real thing in my hands. It is only the architect who can fulfil my dreams according to those simple plans, even if I can help by doing some labouring.

Why, then, do I feel so sure, so often, that I am best qualified to plan my life? Of course I can present my dream to God, but he knows the realities, the practicalities. He can see the bigger picture. He can fulfil my dreams wonderfully, but only when they are submitted to his purpose and transformed by his plans. My dreams need to be made real by the true architect. It is then, and only then, that I can enjoy the living, breathing reality of a life built or restored by him. But still I make plans…

Reflect… 'a personal organizer'

God—I want a personal organizer—
one that will organize me… personally.
There on the front page it will tell me who I am:
my phone, my fax, my e-mail,
in case I lose myself in busyness.
So that I can plan.

Then all the calendars in a line
for ten years ahead and behind,
with the dates all at my fingertips.
So that I can plan.

Next I want a week to view.
I can't have 'tomorrow surprises'.
'At a glance' will be the best.
So that I can plan.

Include some facts and figures.
I need to know how much,
how far, how fast, how certain.
So that I can plan.

The dates that I need listing:
when born, when wed, when ever.
I must know when to send things.
So that I can plan.

A space for some addresses—
business, kids and kin.
I need to know just where they are
So that I can plan.

A few accounting pages
so I can count the money.
(I never know just where it goes!)
So that I can plan.

Then leave some blank pink pages.
Just give me a little space
to write those things that matter.
So that I can plan.

One last page for a memo,
A 'don't forget to do'.
One eye on the future.
So that I can plan.

… And God wrote on the memo page…
'For I know the plans I have for you,'
declares the Lord,
'plans to prosper you and not to harm you,
plans to give you hope
and a future.'

✦

All-knowing God,
Take my rough and ready plans,
my half guesses, assumptions and dreams.
Straighten out my estimates.
Hold your rule against my life.
Remind me of your great design,
still to be completed.
And as I build my life for you, have me follow your plans.

✛

HOW TO TRUST WITHOUT HOLDING YOUR BREATH

GALLERY: 'THE TRAPEZE'

How different in composition this next painting is—a small square canvas, the figures packed tightly into the frame, secure in their space. It is in the style of Degas, the painter of dancers. Before you are two dancers, not of the stage but of the sky. These are the flying stars of the circus, working on the trapeze, swinging from bars and wires high above the crowd.

You can tell from the brush strokes that the picture has been painted with energy and haste, as if the artist needed to paint in the midst of the performance. (Where did he paint from? Did he join them perched in those tarpaulin skies?) Perhaps this was his last chance to record the moment. The bright lights of the circus ring below have been dimmed, the canvas sky above is in shadow, and spotlights pick out the figures. Their facial features are blurred, almost contorted.

Below are more shadows—darkness, with just a few ovals of grey suggesting a crowd, their faces turned upwards, their knuckles gripping the wooden seats beneath them. All eyes are fixed skywards, all breath is held tightly, as tightly as the two performers will need to hold each other once they meet mid-air if that breath is to be released in a sigh of relief rather than as a gasp of fear.

To the left hangs the one who is to be 'picked up' mid-air. The wire attached to his swinging bar is slacker than that of his companion, as he has only just begun his swing, releasing himself from his perch at the perfect moment. Now he dangles perilously, his chalked hands gripping the bar, his body bent in an arc of flight. His white, slightly worn vest and leggings fit close around his frame. His muscular arms are curved, as if he was indeed one of Degas's dancers. Yet, there is no sign of panic, no sign of perspiration, no hint of fear. His body is at ease, as if he were merely waiting in the park. His face is at peace, his jaw is relaxed, but his eyes are fixed on his companion—not in anxiety or in desperation, but in trust.

There is nothing he can do but wait.

His pace and momentum are already set, both by his own judgment and their shared experience. He has nothing to do to ensure a safe meeting mid-air except depend, utterly and completely, on the skill, judgment and strength of the other. So he hangs in the centre of the painting—waiting, caught in time.

His companion, painted to look older, more experienced, has, you assume, been swinging high above the crowd for longer. He has gathered pace, built momentum like a pendulum, his launch perfectly timed, his signal to the other precisely given. It is a signal he has passed and received so many times in this highwire life. His strength is evident, his energy at its height, his body taut and tense, his physique honed like the polished bronze statue of a champion athlete. The upper side of his body is painted lighter, illuminated by the bright beam of the spotlight below. His fingers, splayed and strong, are just a handspan from the ankles of his companion, moments from his grasp. His eyes are fixed on the other's feet, on the paper soles of the dance slippers soiled with chalk and sawdust, and marked by many hours spent on the bars and wires. He has one chance to catch hold of those ankles. It is now or never. If his reach falls short or his grip slackens, his companion will tumble down into the safety net, maybe even on to the sawdust below. But his timing will be perfect, his judgment sure. His grip will hold, because he has so much to lose—because, you realize, as you glance at the painting's title and check the resemblance, this is his son.

In the father, the son is placing his trust, his very life. The artist has chosen to freeze the frame with the trusting and the trusted almost touching, almost joined mid-air, almost reunited—but not quite. This is a hushed, almost unspeakable moment of trust in the darkness. Silently, breath held, you tiptoe away from the picture.

INTRODUCTION

Faith and trust go hand in hand through any period of waiting, enjoying a mutually supportive and nurturing relationship. Faith supports trust and trust encourages faith. In a sense, faith is waiting. It is certainly illustrated as such in the lives of those we read about last week. When Abraham 'believed God' he was, quite simply, trusting him. When Mary accepted God's plans for her life and the life of her son, she trusted those plans because they were God's. When Joseph risked his own record of integrity and the reputation of the young woman to whom he was betrothed, he trusted God for much more than the future of his family.

Trust inevitably involves waiting to see what God will do, but we're not trusting if we hold our breath until he does it. Although trust is one of the first skills we must develop as we learn the art of waiting, every one of us knows that waiting in trust is easier said than done. Yet trust, like any artist's skill, gains in strength and ease of application with practice, developing into a solid and mature accomplishment. Over the next week, we will spend some time considering the nature of trust, why we find it so difficult, and how we can benefit from a bit more practice.

Most of us worry, even if we don't admit it, but Paul didn't. He saw no need and no point in it. For Paul, feelings, faith and focus were the key to avoiding worry. He did not waste time considering the 'what if's of life as we do. Instead of making little forays into the future to check the route, he was happy to let God set the path.

Very often, we do follow Paul's advice, and pray. In fact, we can spend quite a lot of time in prayer meetings. Sometimes, though, when God does answer our prayers, honour our trust and end our waiting, we can hardly believe our ears, let alone our eyes. That's what happened at the prayer meeting Rhoda was part of (Acts 12:5–17). God answered the prayers of those gathered to pray for

Peter's release, but they didn't believe it when Peter appeared at the door, freed from prison.

It always comforts me somewhat that the disciples were such slow learners! Despite the fact that they had Jesus in their midst or nearby, they still worried. In fact, they made themselves absolutely terrified, and only pulled themselves together when Jesus made it clear that he was 'in the same boat' and in control (Mark 6:45–52). On another occasion it was Jesus who kept his friends waiting, teaching them something of his Father's perspective on life and death in the process. Martha and Mary discovered that perspective changes everything, and that they had to learn to adopt a heavenly view (John 11:22). The sisters knew what it was to wait in anxiety for the sake of someone that they loved. Husband and father David Noble shares something of that waiting for the sake of a loved one later in the week.

To end this section, we take a new look at a familiar psalm, the 23rd, revisiting this great song of trust from four different personal perspectives. As you read each one, make fresh observations and gain new insights into your own walk with the good shepherd.

DON'T WORRY, BE HAPPY!

Do not be anxious about anything, but in everything, by prayer and petition, with thanksgiving, present your requests to God. And the peace of God, which transcends all understanding, will guard your hearts and your minds in Christ Jesus. Finally, brothers, whatever is true, whatever is noble, whatever is right, whatever is pure, whatever is lovely, whatever is admirable—if anything is excellent or praiseworthy—think about such things. Whatever you have learned or received or heard from me—put it into practice.

PHILIPPIANS 4:6–9

Paul sent this joyful 'thank you' letter from prison back to the church in Philippi with Epaphroditus, who had earlier delivered a special gift from the church members to him. Not one to miss an opportunity, Paul takes time to give a bit of practical advice too. The wonderful words contained in these verses are especially poignant. If Paul could write with such conviction while imprisoned and waiting for an uncomfortable meeting with the emperor Nero, his letter must have been powerfully encouraging for the Philippian Christians. Paul certainly wasn't pacing his cell as far as his chains would allow while he waited. He was waiting in peace, assured of God's provision and able to share something of both with his friends.

The letter is simple and straightforward. Not a shadow of doubt falls on Paul's pages: his feelings are flooded with peace, his faith is strong, his focus is clear. He encourages the Philippian Christians to 'wait' in the same way, and to do more than just 'look on the bright side'. In fact, he gives them a checklist of the best things to think about. If we had to paraphrase Paul's words briefly for today, we might be tempted to conclude that he wrote, 'Don't worry, be happy!'

Worry is almost second nature to most of us, perhaps especially those of us who are parents. Rarely do we have to decide that we will worry, but we nearly always have to decide not to. I love the proverb that reminds us, 'Worry is like a rocking chair—it gives you something to do, but it doesn't get you anywhere!' Some of us enjoy worrying so much that we worry when we don't have anything to worry about. 'What's happened?' we ask ourselves as our metaphorical rocking chair comes to a standstill. 'Why am I not worried?' Then it's not long before we're oiling those rockers with the lubricant of anxiety and happily tipping to and fro to nowhere.

Paul's good advice for the Philippian Christians is not to worry about anything. He doesn't say, as we often do, 'Try not to worry'; just 'Don't'—about anything. Paul wouldn't have had time for the rocking chair. He would have seen it quite simply as a pointless activity. 'Why worry,' we can hear him say, 'when you can pray?'

Of course, that's the next thing to do: 'present your requests to God'. In other words, let him know what you need, and tell him what it is you're worried about—not with desperate pleas, waves of panic or hand-wringing doubt, but with thanksgiving. We might seriously doubt Paul's sanity at this point. 'What is he on?' we cry! Notice, though, that it's after prayer and thanksgiving, not before, that Paul assures us that we will know God's peace. Once the whole situation is in God's hands, surrendered to his control, wrapped in our thankfulness for his provision and care, we can be at peace.

A day or two before I wrote this chapter, I knew for myself a perfect practical illustration of that peace. I was scheduled to attend an important meeting in Cardiff, and needed to leave Devon on a very early train. As is often the case with teenagers, my 16-year-old daughter had woken feeling low and angry. As I waited for the taxi to take me to the station, she announced that she could not face going to school and was staying in bed. Furious at the timing, and furious with her, I had no choice but to jump in the taxi to catch the train, leaving her behind and wondering what on earth would happen. I sat on the train fretting and worrying, sending her text messages on my mobile phone to 'keep her company' and to try to lift her mood. I had little response, just a grunted text word or two, like 's'pose', or 'whatever'.

Finally, a bit slow on the uptake, I remembered Paul's advice, and prayed. My prayer was certainly heartfelt. I definitely presented my requests to God: 'Please keep her in your arms, Lord!' I thanked him for her, and for the good days, and for all the potential he has given her. I tried to put into practice 'all I had learned'. I also asked for wisdom regarding the contents of the next text message I would send. In it, I suggested she sleep during the morning, then perhaps watch one of our favourite mum-and-daughter 'feel good' films on video—preferably one filled with positive, 'life-enriching' words that would lift her heart (although, of course, I didn't phrase it quite like that to her). I suggested a title and, as I couldn't be there, asked God to watch with her (if he could bear it)!

As I sent the message, I felt peaceful at last. By the middle of the afternoon, she was text-messaging little snippets of the film's dialogue to me, both the lines that made her laugh and the incidents she knew I'd love to be reminded of. We both knew that peace of God which is beyond understanding. More than that, I had unknowingly suggested she follow Paul's final piece of advice, because, 'finally', Paul suggests that we maintain that perfect peace by filling our minds with less of the 'whatever will happen?' and more of the 'whatever is lovely'.

'Take your mind off it,' we might say. 'Take it off the worry, and on to something pure, lovely, admirable and praiseworthy.' The benefit of that advice lifted both my daughter's heart and mine until we could be together again to talk things through. Paul's advice was good advice!

Reflect...

Paul's wait was characterized by three things: emotions flooded with peace, a faith that was strong, and a focus that was clear. Use those characteristics as you pray for whatever is worrying you today.

BUT WHAT IF...?

'Therefore I tell you, do not worry about your life, what you will eat or drink; or about your body, what you will wear. Is not life more important than food, and the body more important than clothes? Look up at the birds of the air; they do not sow or reap or store away in barns, and yet your heavenly Father feeds them. Are you not much more valuable than they? Who of you by worrying can add a single hour to his life?

'And why do you worry about clothes? See how the lilies of the field grow. They do not labour or spin. Yet I tell you that not even Solomon in all his splendour was dressed like one of these. If that is how God clothes the grass of the field, which is here today and tomorrow is thrown into the fire, will he not much more clothe you, O you of little faith? So do not worry, saying, "What shall we eat?" or "What shall we drink?" or "What shall we wear?" For the pagans run after all these things, and your heavenly Father knows that you need them. But seek first his kingdom and his righteousness, and all these things will be given to you as well. Therefore do not worry about tomorrow, for tomorrow will worry about itself. Each day has enough trouble of its own.'

MATTHEW 6:25–34

For Christmas last year, a friend of mine was given a book called *What If?*[3] It re-evaluates military history and cleverly, sometimes chillingly, suggests what might have happened if wars had been lost instead of won, and toppled tyrants had remained in power. It's a fascinating and useful book for amateur historians, but it made me wonder how healthy it is to wonder 'what might have been' in other contexts. Our 'what if?'s can all too easily become a form of worry in reverse.

Perhaps we're more inclined, though, to apply a 'What if...?' question to the future. 'What if I don't get this job...? What if we can't find somewhere to live? What if the test results are bad?' If we don't know what lies ahead, we want at least to test out the various alternatives in our imagination as part of a coping strategy. It's as if we catapult ourselves into an uncertain future to test the water of 'not knowing'.

It's this 'not knowing' that is so difficult. Most of us fear the unknown, and that's what makes it so difficult to trust God with our future. Few of us like uncertainty. People are fascinated by knowing what the future holds—as if today didn't 'have enough worry of its own'. That's why the horoscopes page is often the first a reader will turn to in a newspaper or magazine, and why the last few years have seen a rise in the publication of mainstream magazines offering 'personal predictions' about what lies ahead. Yet this kind of forecasting can lead to a deeper fear of the future rather than faith in the one true God who knows what it holds.

Perhaps our interest in the future is the flipside of the fact that we are designed to look forward to the hope that we have in God, and all he has prepared for us, but it's often hard to do that without making assumptions about what God might have planned or what the outcome of any situation might be. If we're finding it difficult to trust God for what lies in the future, we can often try to send an imaginary scout ahead to see what's coming. We squint into the distance for a sign of anything that will assure us that what lies ahead is OK. Yet the scout may bring back the wrong impression, sending us into wilder panic, or we may strain our eyes looking up our life's road for landmarks, instead of concentrating on where we are now.

Is it any wonder we so often trip up? Often it's this very step and the next that God wants us to focus on. We can be so busy looking ahead that we 'can't see for looking' when God wants us to pay attention to what is under our nose, now. In effect, we are making little forays into the future to check it out for bumps and hazards, forgetting that God holds that future, including the rough ground, as securely as he holds the present and the past. 'God only knows,' we say, and indeed it is only God who knows. We cannot, and should not, predict what he might do, except in joyous anticipation of the fulfilment of each tiny part of his plan, and in the confident knowledge that whatever he does will be the very best for us.

As I write, our family is contemplating a move from Devon in the south-west of England to Kent or Sussex in the south-east. It would mean a major upheaval for our two teenage children at crucial points in their school careers and a big change in lifestyle and location for all of us. It's not that I mind moving. I'm one of those strange individuals who enjoy change. It's just that I want to get those changes organized. I want to know that the children will get places in the schools they've chosen, that we will find a house in the area nearby, and that I won't pine terribly for the West Country we love so much or long for the screech of seagulls. I have been 'squinting into the distance' like mad!

Just recently, a friend quite inadvertently challenged me. Not knowing how anxious I had been, she made me realize, through her obvious delight at our 'exciting' plans, that I had been dwelling solely on the negatives. I had been thinking more about the problems and the hurdles to be overcome than the opportunities God was placing in our path. My friend's response has made it easier for me to know at least some excitement as to what God might have in store for us.

Perhaps we never clearly see the delicate line of God's guidance until we look behind us, but however invisible that line may seem as we look ahead, it is being clearly drawn by a God who loves us. I recently heard Rico Tice, writer of the popular *Christianity Explored* course, say simply, 'Jesus is the most loving man who ever lived.' If we can't trust our future to the most loving man who ever lived, who can we trust? We may not know what the future holds, but we know who holds the future.

Reflect...

Does the way I live day to day reveal who I believe holds my future?

Lord of yesterday,
Lord of this moment,
Lord of tomorrow,
Teach me to trust your timing.

STORMY WEATHER

Immediately Jesus made his disciples get into the boat and go ahead of him to Bethsaida, while he dismissed the crowd. After leaving them, he went up on a mountainside to pray. When evening came, the boat was in the middle of the lake, and he was alone on land. He saw the disciples straining at the oars, because the wind was against them. About the fourth watch of the night he went out to them, walking on the lake. He was about to pass by them, but when they saw him walking on the lake, they thought he was a ghost. They cried out, because they all saw him and were terrified. Immediately he spoke to them and said, 'Take courage! It is I. Don't be afraid.' Then he climbed into the boat with them, and the wind died down. They were completely amazed, for they had not understood about the loaves; their hearts were hardened.

MARK 6:45–52

Sometimes our wait is for something more life-changing or life-threatening than just a move to another part of the country. When it is, we may feel as if we wait above a precipice and daren't look down. Our waiting place then becomes a barren place where we feel as if we stand totally alone and more exposed than we have ever been. But God is closer than we realize.

Earlier in the day, just before the events of our Bible reading, Jesus had met the needs of thousands of hungry people on the hillside by miraculously providing their lunch, demonstrating to his disciples that he was concerned with the most simple of needs. But they had 'not understood about the loaves' (v. 52). They were slow to learn!

As evening came, he sent those same disciples on ahead across the water to Bethsaida, while he went to a quiet place to pray. Yet it seems that he kept an eye on them from the shore, watching them as the weather got worse and the storm grew. Soon they were in the midst of panic, and had almost forgotten him. He came near them, as if to pass by, perhaps to give them the opportunity of calling out to him for help. Yet they didn't recognize him. This was the second time that they had needed Jesus in the midst of a storm. The first time he had been sleeping in the boat with them, yet still they were terrified, and now here they are again. Similar scenario, similar storm, similar silliness—and with Jesus close by, quietly splashing about to help! It's as if Jesus sighs and says, 'OK, I'll give these very slow learners a second chance. Surely they will remember that as long as I am near they are safe?' They didn't, of course. They had put him out of their minds, let fear fix itself firmly in his place and were now suffering as a consequence.

We can hardly 'tut-tut' at these feeble sailors, because we are so similar. We so easily forget Jesus' past protection and faithfulness in the midst of a storm of new fears. It was only when Jesus climbed into the boat with them that the storm calmed down, leaving the disciples still bewildered, still unable to recognize fully the saviour in their midst, and still not understanding about the miraculous picnic of bread and fish—or the calming of the waves. We can imagine the sad frustration of Jesus. He must have loved them so much at such moments. How he longed to make them understand, but he knew they would need to learn the hard way.

In the same way, God will sometimes send us on, apparently alone, into difficult situations. We should never forget, though, that, like Jesus on the shore, he never takes his eyes off us. I believe that he will sometimes wait to see whether we will turn to him in dependence and trust before stepping in to help. Trusting him in the midst of our fear should be a simple lesson to learn, but is often the most difficult. Sometimes it isn't until we have nowhere else to go, no other way of confronting or managing our fear, that we will trust God. Our faces may be slapped by the waves, our arms tired from struggling with the oars, before we will recognize that he has drawn close to us, almost passing us by in an effort to secure our dependence and trust when it matters most.

When Jesus finally did act, he acted 'immediately' (vv. 45–50). This reminds us that he may ask us to learn by waiting, but he will never allow us to wait a moment longer than is necessary before coming to our aid. He isn't playing some kind of cynical testing game, but drawing our attention to the fact that if we called on him first, we could save ourselves the worst of the struggle against the storm. Then, because he cannot bear to leave us in the midst of our fear and bewilderment a moment longer, Jesus climbs into the boat with us. The storm may not always die down. Sometimes it may continue to rage, even overwhelm us, but we need not fear— because he is in the boat with us, just as he will climb 'inside' every detail of our lives if we will just invite him.

Hilary McDowell, a writer and speaker born with great physical disabilities alongside greater creative abilities and with a marvellous love of life, writes, 'Given back to God, any negatives can be transformed into the positive which he had originally intended... In my experience he fulfils his potential for our lives, not necessarily by removing the difficulties, but by climbing inside them with us, and transforming them from within.'[4]

Reflect...

When have you felt God asking you to 'go on ahead' alone into the wind and waves of your life? How have you been aware of his watching from the shore?

At what point has he entered your situation and transformed it from within? How might those 'wind and wave' experiences help you wait in trust in the midst of future storms?

Lord, when I am in the midst of the storms of life,
remind me that you are watching over me.
When I wrestle with the waves, you will take the oars.
When the tides of life threaten to engulf me,
you can calm them with a word.
Though I take my eyes from you in the midst of my fear,
you do not lose sight of me, but will walk towards me through the storm,
and climb into my life beside me.

WAITING FOR SOMEONE?

Now a man named Lazarus was sick. He was from Bethany, the village of Mary and her sister Martha. This Mary, whose brother Lazarus now lay sick, was the same one who poured perfume on the Lord and wiped his feet with her hair. So the sisters sent word to Jesus, 'Lord, the one you love is sick.' When he heard this, Jesus said, 'This sickness will not end in death. No, it is for God's glory so that God's Son may be glorified through it.' Jesus loved Martha and her sister and Lazarus. Yet when he heard that Lazarus was sick, he stayed where he was two more days...

'Lord,' Martha said to Jesus, 'if you had been here, my brother would not have died. But I know that even now God will give you whatever you ask.'

JOHN 11:1–6, 21–22

'How could Jesus be late?' I can imagine Mary and Martha fretting and wringing their hands (perhaps, according to character, one more discreetly than the other) and looking along the road with increasing desperation. They are waiting so hopefully for Jesus to appear and heal their brother Lazarus. They have seen him restore others to health and wholeness so many times before, and Lazarus is his friend—Jesus would surely want to heal him. So why the delay?

Can't you just imagine too the cynical taunts of the neighbours? 'Well, he's not here, is he?' (with a knowing nod). 'He might be your friend, but he doesn't turn up when you need him, does he?' (gossip, gossip, mumble, mumble). 'Well, I mean, you just can't get the friends these days, can you?' The gossips slip away, some hurrying their inquisitive and dawdling children on ahead of them. Those nearest settle themselves in the doorways of houses to watch what happens next.

Mary must have turned away, hurt and anxious, wondering where this dear trusted friend could possibly be, and why he would apparently abandon them in such a heartless way. Martha must have tried to busy herself to hide her anger and frustration, constantly asking questions that found no answers.

Jesus must have found it equally hard to wait before joining his friends, knowing their anxiety, especially when they had specifically sent for him. He had to trust their sorrowing hearts to his Father, in much the same way that they were being asked to trust him. There was a much wider purpose for their wait than they could understand.

When Jesus does finally arrive, despite the fact that Lazarus is dead, Martha at least gives a hint that she believes that nothing is impossible for God. She renews her trust in Jesus with the words, 'But I know that even now God will give you whatever you ask' (v. 22). She dares to believe that this man can raise her brother back to life, despite the decay of Lazarus' body during the days in the tomb. How amazed she must have been when Jesus explained the very essence of his life and ministry to her, with the words, 'I am the resurrection and the life'. He goes on to reunite the risen Lazarus with his sisters in one of the most breathtaking demonstrations of God's power, compassion and purpose recorded in the Gospels. Now that was something worth waiting for!

One Christmas Eve when our first child was very new, I lay awake at my in-laws' home, waiting for my husband to return from an annual supper with schoolfriends. The roads were icy, he had been somewhat unwise to make the journey and the later it became, the more concerned I grew. Our baby daughter was sleeping in her basket next to the bed, and when I reached out to her I found that her hands were icy too, so I lifted her into bed with me for warmth, all the time waiting for her father to join us in safety. I felt very vulnerable with this tiny cold child and all my fears. Eventually he arrived, way beyond the midnight hour, without a care in the world and oblivious to my anxiety. He had just got chatting and forgotten the time. We had not been married long and I needed to learn not to worry, but even now, 17 years later, I am only slowly learning the lesson. Over those years he has often been similarly late. I have grown gradually more concerned, and it is usually at about the time I imagine him badly injured at the roadside, alone at a remote spot or even in the hospital morgue that his key will turn in the lock and he will appear with a wide grin—still, after all these years, oblivious to the worry he has caused!

There is a difference between waiting for someone we know well and someone we know only vaguely. If we are waiting for a business associate, we may assume they have been held up at another appointment. We may feel frustrated at the waste of time, or wonder whom we should contact, but our emotions are not deeply engaged. If, however, we are waiting for someone we know well, love and trust, we ask questions that can tear at our hearts. Like Martha and Mary, we may feel let down, forgotten, abandoned. 'Why won't they come?' we ask; 'Where are they?'—even, 'Don't I matter?'

It can sometimes feel like that with God. We may have been expecting him to act, just as Martha and Mary expected Jesus, and then we become bewildered by his apparent distance and silence. We shouldn't stop trusting him, though. He may be asking us to trust him just that little bit more—perhaps way beyond the darkest, coldest midnight hour.

Reflect...

He does not forget us: 'I will not forget you! See, I have engraved you on the palms of my hands' (Isaiah 49:15–16).

Father God, remind me that though you may ask me to wait for you, you will not forget me. But sometimes you will ask me to trust you to appear at the time of your choosing. I may feel alone—but I am not deserted. I may feel lost—but you will find me. My wait for you will never be in vain, even if I wait in the dark... and beyond the midnight hour.

'WELL, WHAT WERE YOU EXPECTING?'

So Peter was kept in prison, but the church was earnestly praying to God for him... Then Peter came to himself and said, 'Now I know without a doubt that the Lord sent his angel and rescued me from Herod's clutches and from everything the Jewish people were anticipating.' When this had dawned on him, he went to the house of Mary the mother of John, also called Mark, where many people had gathered and were praying. Peter knocked at the outer entrance, and a servant girl named Rhoda came to answer the door. When she recognized Peter's voice, she was so overjoyed she ran back without opening it and exclaimed, 'Peter is at the door!'

'You're out of your mind,' they told her. When she kept insisting that it was so, they said, 'It must be his angel.' But Peter kept on knocking, and when they opened the door and saw him, they were astonished.

ACTS 12:5, 11–16

Here is little Rhoda, perhaps excused from her maid's duties for a while to join in the prayer meeting. A number of members of the early Church have gathered together to pray earnestly for Peter, who is in prison; and Rhoda sits, maybe, at the edge of the group, half in awe and half in fear, listening to their prayers. They hear a knock on the door, and Rhoda leaps to her feet and goes, full of trepidation, to open it. Might this knock mean more arrests? Was she herself in danger? Meanwhile, those at the prayer meeting continue praying and waiting for something to happen... preferably Peter's miraculous release.

Suddenly Rhoda is hot-footing it back into their midst with

excited claims that Peter is at the door—and what do they do? Promptly tell her she's nuts! The very thing they were waiting and praying for had happened and they didn't believe it! Why couldn't they believe that such a thing could actually happen?

Thankfully, God does not always wait for our faith to be demonstrated before he acts to help us. He loves surprising us—for that is surely what he did here. I wonder how much longer poor Peter had to wait outside before somebody let him in.

We laugh at the sitcom hilarity of this lovely scene but, like the group at the prayer meeting, we may not expect or even really want what we're waiting and praying for. How would we feel if we actually received it?

Every year at film and television awards, at least one winner will give a predictable speech: 'I've waited all my life for this,' they say, the tears flowing. 'I can't believe it's happening!' They stand on stage in a posh frock or sharp suit designed for the occasion, hair immaculate, outfit bejewelled by a style consultant and clutching the heavy award to their breast—but they still can't believe that what they've waited for has actually happened. All too often, we can be like that when we pray. We will ask for something and, even though we are confident that God would want it too, we are astounded when he stretches out his hands to offer us that very thing. I believe that if it were possible, we would look heavenward and see a wry smile on God's face, a twinkle in his eye, and hear the playful question, 'Well? What did you expect?'

Mark was a young student member of a church I once attended, whose prayer life gained quite a reputation. He had developed a personal ministry among the homeless of the city, sharing his small allowance with them and buying blankets, food and hot drinks for his friends on the street. He was left with virtually nothing to meet his own needs, yet he took God at his word and prayed, trusting in God daily to provide everything from meals to clothing and books for his studies. He never went short, and his needs were met in the most amazing ways—just as he expected.

I can remember the words of a mutual friend who was part of

Mark's prayer group. He said, 'You have to look out when you pray with Mark. When he asks, he gets what he asks for! And he doesn't often have to wait long.' Perhaps God honoured the fact that Mark was dependent on him to supply not only his own needs but also the needs of others. Mark knew that his material needs were few, but that his most powerful resources—prayer, and trust in God's provision according to his word—could provide more than he and his friends would ever need.

It's often we who complicate matters. We stand alongside others who are going through a difficult time and ask, 'What can we do to help?' Then we may feel frustrated when they say, 'Just pray'. It seems as if we are being given the second-class helping job, the one that doesn't get our hands dirty or get us too close to the action. What we don't realize is that praying is far more than 'just' praying. It is the ultimate act of trust. It is 'just' about the best thing we can possibly do for anyone in any situation while we wait for God to act. What else can we do that gives us all the resources of heaven at our disposal, Jesus on our side, and the Holy Spirit as counsellor—the one who even provides for us the words to pray?

So if you're waiting, don't just stand there—pray something! God might just open a door and surprise you!

Reflect...

Rejoice in thankfulness at those times when God has said, 'Well, what did you expect?'

Lord, as I wait and pray, prepare me for your 'open doors', and give me a spirit of expectancy, for you delight in meeting my needs when I depend wholly on you.

DAVID: A HUSBAND IN WAITING

I lift up my eyes to the hills—
where does my help come from?
My help comes from the Lord,
the Maker of heaven and earth.

PSALM 121:1–2

David Noble lives with his wife, Caroline, and young children, Alex and Eve, near Ely, Cambridgeshire. Married for 13 years, David and Caroline became Christians through an Alpha course in May 2000. Caroline is a nurse by profession and David is a commercial director for a multi-national clinical trials company and an Anglican Reader (lay preacher). This is David's waiting story, in his own words.

'When Wendy asked me to write about the waiting surrounding Caroline's diagnosis with breast cancer, I wasn't quite sure where to start. We seem to have been waiting for something almost continually since the day she was diagnosed. But it's not like any other kind of waiting, because our whole life has been affected by it. When the diagnosis came, it was a huge shock—totally out of the blue.

'Although there was an intense sense of urgency, it took two weeks to get through all the tests before the treatment could start. The result of each test had to be waited for. I felt frightened, helpless and unsure of everything as we waited to hear what the doctors had found. Finally, the tests were complete and we could meet with the consultant to decide on a course of action for Caroline's treatment. The last of the tests (the MRI)—the one we had waited longest for—had shown that there were some lymph nodes testing positive, and this meant that Caroline qualified for the clinical trial of a new advanced treatment. It was during this time that we rediscovered a well-known piece of scripture: "Therefore do not worry about tomorrow, for tomorrow will worry about itself" (Matthew 6:34). On the face of it, this appears to be a very good piece of advice from Jesus, but when you try to put it into practice you realize how hard it is to trust him and give that worry over to God, letting him take care of it.

'After the longest two weeks of my life, Caroline was finally able to begin treatment. I couldn't begin to describe how I felt, sitting next to her as she started the first of six cycles of chemotherapy. I sat and chatted to her as the drip that she was connected to fed a toxic mix of chemicals into her bloodstream, chemicals that we hoped would kill the cancer cells but at the same time would make her feel awful.

'"Who of you by worrying can add a single hour to his life?" (Matthew 6:27). I'm sure no one would think that worrying would make them live longer, but trying not to worry about a loved one who is having such drastic treatment is very difficult. So I waited and I worried! I waited for Caroline to begin to get better, knowing that she would appear to get worse first. I waited for the inevitable tiredness to hit her and I tried to keep things going at home until it passed.

'Eventually, after six cycles, the chemotherapy phase was over. Miraculously, the large tumour mass had disappeared, but now we faced more waiting. Although the tumour had visibly "gone", it was unlikely to have been totally destroyed. We'd talked about the next stage for some time, and Caroline appeared to be well prepared for surgery, a mastectomy and removal of lymph nodes. However, before the surgery could go ahead, we had to wait a few weeks to allow Caroline to recover. It was, on the one hand, a good few weeks—Caroline was less tired and could do a little more (if I let her!)—but on the other hand it was a time of more worry. I was concerned that with such an aggressive cancer, even a few weeks without treatment would give it an opportunity to get a foothold again, and I was worried for Caroline as she prepared for surgery that no woman should have to think about.

'Finally, the day of the operation arrived. I'll never forget how relaxed Caroline was: the Lord truly gave her peace and calm on that day. I waited again. Friends did their best to occupy me and keep me company while Caroline was in theatre but, although I greatly appreciated their efforts, nothing could stop me thinking about her. At 9.30pm the hospital called with a message from Caroline: "Tell him I love him, and tell him to stop worrying and go and get some sleep!" Ever-practical advice from my dear wife!

'The next wait was for pathology results of tissue removed during surgery. As Caroline had her operation just before Christmas, it looked as though we wouldn't get the results until after the holidays —but the Lord sent us a special Christmas present that year. On 23 December we were told that no living cancer cells had been found. These results would, of course, have been just the same had I not worried!

'Despite chemotherapy, surgery, radiotherapy and continuing antibody treatment, we are still waiting. During the first few months it was hard not to think about the cancer coming back. Two years later, we are waiting for more research to be made available, in the hope that this will help us decide when it will be safe to stop treatment. So we're still waiting.

'The further away we get from the diagnosis date, the greater the odds are against the cancer returning. Yet, paradoxically, the further away we get, the more intense my worries become. They are less frequent, but because our lives are as "normal" as they will ever be, even the remotest possibility of going back is hard to contemplate. We continue to take strength from Matthew 6:34, and we trust in the Lord, give our worries over to him, and wait to see what he has in store for us next.'

Reflect...

When was your longest wait for a loved one? How did God wait with you?

Father God, when we are waiting in the realities of pain and fear, help us to find you... through the whisper of your love in the silence, with the candle-like flame of your hope in the darkness, and in the warmth of your arms in the cold light of day.

A WALK WITH THE SHEPHERD

Psalm 23 is without a doubt the most well-known psalm in the Bible. Many of us grew up with it, sang it in a variety of versions, may even have it printed on tea towels or coffee mugs. While its familiarity can be comforting, we can easily think that, because we know it so well, there can't possibly be anything more we can learn from it. Yet Psalm 23 is the ultimate psalm of trust and, during difficult times of waiting, it can transform our experience if we look for new meaning in its well-loved lines.

> The Lord is my shepherd, I shall not be in want.
> He makes me lie down in green pastures,
> he leads me beside quiet waters,
> he restores my soul.
> He guides me in paths of righteousness
> for his name's sake.
> Even though I walk
> through the valley of the shadow of death,
> I will fear no evil,
> for you are with me;
> your rod and staff, they comfort me.
> You prepare a table before me
> in the presence of my enemies.
> You anoint my head with oil;
> my cup overflows.
> Surely goodness and love will follow me
> all the days of my life,
> and I will dwell in the house of the Lord for ever.

It is difficult to shake off the traditional view of Jesus as shepherd complete with flowing grass-stain-free robe and carrying a fluffy lamb in his arms. But we can develop a fresh perception of elements of the psalm by paraphrasing it, so that we can apply it more effectively in our everyday lives.

Here, the 23rd Psalm is brought to God in four short monologues from a teenager, a parent of small children, a businessman and a newly retired woman. As you read each one, ask God to speak clearly into your own personal circumstances and draw attention to elements of your own relationship with him as shepherd.

Sam (aged 16, likes surfing, music and girls)

I'm glad you're the boss.
I can lie on my bed, earphones in, staring at the ceiling,
but I'm not alone. No moodies. Just you in the music.
Picking me up, making me feel great—just by being there with me.
I can ask you which way to go—
if I should say 'Yes' or 'Whatever' or just walk—
and you let me know.
And even when I'm on the edge of the scary stuff, you're ahead of me.
I can't be fazed by it, because you're there to stick up for me,
to nudge and wallop the enemy on my behalf,
to get me back into the light again
and give me a Dad-hug of reassurance.
And then we party while they look on!
And the great thing is that all the time you're out in front,
checking the route,
things can only get better and better—for ever.

A parent (tired… as ever)

Now I understand a little of how you feel as a parent to me!
You anticipate my needs as I do theirs.
You love me, whatever,
and you ensure I get the rest I need, even if it's in snatches.
You find me a few quiet moments with you if I ask for them—
just enough to press on,
drawing on your strength.
These little ones, what extremes of emotion they produce—fierce love,
inexplicable fear, fragile vulnerability.
But your greater love protects, guides, and knows what is best for them—
more than I ever will.
You're walking this parenting walk with me.
They are carried high on your shoulders
and in your arms as well as mine…
and they always will be.

Tom (a pre-meeting brief)

Would you chair this meeting, Lord?
Remind me what the priorities are, tick down the agenda, steer the debate.
I need these few moments of peace before you,
because I want to arrive at decisions your way, with integrity;
develop policy with compassion.
I don't want to be swayed by those who look for personal gain,
or overlook the needs of the more vulnerable who have no voice here.
Lord, as my shepherd, guard what is right,
fend off attack, show me the way through,
and hook me out of any tight corners I might get myself into.
There are enemies around that table—
those who would oppose your will—
but I have the assurance that you have chosen me, anointed me,
to be your representative in this place.
Help me to go your way, investing in a future that lasts.

Frances (newly retired, living alone)

You've provided for me so well, Lord, and now my working life is done.
I should be looking forward to all this—
a time for rest, relaxation, peace—and I am.
Now I have time—more time for you, for those you love.
But...
I am fearful too, fearful of what lies ahead,
of what this next stage in my life means.
Remind me that you and I can develop a closer walk
in what are the green pastures,
that as the years move on, your protection and care will be all that I need.
There will be uncertainties, anxieties,
shadows creeping across the edges of my path,
but I have the assurance that my ultimate destination is home...
and that there is still much celebration to be enjoyed with you on the way.

✤

DON'T JUST SIT THERE!
DO SOMETHING!

GALLERY: 'WAYS OF WAITING'

You go through a doorway in the gallery and walk across a shiny wooden floor towards a sculpture group. These figures are large, white and simply carved, without facial features or detail. They are life-size, mostly seated.

You had assumed it was a single group of eight figures but, as you move closer, you notice that there is some distance between two groups of four—as if the sculptor wanted to show a mildly busy moment on a station platform.

To the left, a group of three is seated, together, yet separate, and apparently unaware of one another. The nearest of the three seems about to stand. The body is turned away, the head looking vaguely in the direction of the second group, as if unsettled, uncertain. As you draw closer you see that, within this first group, the figures are not together in any real sense. They are isolated, positioned as if unaware of each other's presence, each one locked in a private world. The stone is shadowed, rendering it almost grey, brittle, like pumice. The second figure in the group sits with head in hands as if in despair, elbows drawn forwards, shoulders sunk. The sculptor has left huge lumps of stone at knee level, piled like baggage as if to act as an anchor.

A short distance away, the fourth figure sits with legs drawn to one side, as if reluctant to move, like a man in a train seat he has not reserved—wrongly seated, unqualified, but unprepared to surrender to one who is. The vast rounded shape of this last figure is sprawled across as much space as the other three together. It looks abandoned to sleep, head back, the suggestion of a mouth open, oblivious to the wait.

The sight of this group disturbs you. You instinctively want to push the heavy figures together, turn faces towards each other. You want to wake the sleeper, clap your hands to draw the attention of each to another. You want to suggest they get moving, do something, say something—anything to break the silence, not just of the gallery but of the emptiness portrayed. The silence has become part of them, as they have become part of the silence. Their waiting in this place is painful.

Several steps away, the other group of four figures has been positioned. The white stone of these shapes is honey-coloured by the glow of a downlighter. The light softens the shapes, caresses the curves and warms the overall form, as if anointing them with oil... and then you notice that this is not four pieces of stone, but one, seamless and complete.

In this huge single piece, there is life. The figures sit together. Three heads are bent; one is thrown back, not in sleep but in laughter, exclamation, amazement or sheer joy. One is closer to his neighbour, his hand on a forearm. The third is focused on the fourth, as if explaining or teaching, maybe even reaching the punch line of a joke. You sense that there are a hundred things they could be saying to one another.

There is no silence in the way this stone has been carved. Its form speaks. It sings with comfort, encouragement and anticipation all sculpted in glorious interaction. Like the first group, the figures may wait some time, but they have words to say to each other, things to do for each other and places to go with each other in the meantime. They will not mind waiting for a time. In fact, you would like to wait with them a while...

INTRODUCTION

In his autobiography, *Cider with Rosie*, author Laurie Lee tells an amusing (and well-known) story about his first day at school. On entering the hustle and bustle of the classroom as a new boy, he is hastily told, 'Sit here for the present'. Young Laurie does as he is told, but goes home disappointed. When his mother asks him what he thought of school, he proclaims that he will not be going tomorrow. Concerned at her son's short academic life, his mother asks why. 'They told me to sit there for the present,' he wails. 'I waited all day, and no one ever gave me a present.'[5]

Of course, that story reveals most about the difference between adults' and children's use and understanding of language, but it also tells us how our expectations and activity while we wait can make quite a difference, both to the outcome and to the waiting period itself.

This week we'll be taking some time to consider what God would have us do as we wait, and how our obedience—the next skill to develop in the art of waiting—should mean that we don't end up quite as disillusioned as young Laurie Lee.

Most of us understand that if we want to walk forward in a more-or-less straight line, it's a good idea to look where we're going. If we lose our point of focus, we lose not only our way but also our balance. That principle is just as relevant to our spiritual lives. If we keep our eyes fixed on God, we won't lose our bearings. So, to begin with, we have to behave a little like a member of an orchestra—instrument ready, eyes on the conductor, ready to follow every nuance and signal.

Most of us don't like to waste time while waiting. I've already mentioned my habit of always taking plenty to do whenever a wait is likely, but there have also been times when I've put aside those 'things to do' because a chance for conversation has come my way, and I don't want to miss any opportunity God might give me through it. I can't say I'm always willing, but life-changing conversations can happen if we look for them. Neither does 'doing something' always mean frenetic activity and rush. Each of us needs time out for rest and relaxation, and to renew the focus that is so vital for our spiritual balance. It's easy to assume, though, that we need beautiful surroundings and an immaculately prepared Quiet Day or retreat to make that 'time out' worthwhile. As helpful as such days are, time out with God can be found in familiar places right where we are, if only we know where to look and how to listen.

The early Church built community as it waited, serving and loving one another and meeting one another's practical needs—and so can we. A warm, welcoming church family that genuinely cares for the community it serves, both inside and outside the church, doesn't waste time twiddling its waiting thumbs!

Last, but by no means least, we are encouraged to wait in thanksgiving (Philippians 4:6). A thankful heart is a healthy heart. Thankfulness has the built-in advantage of reminding us of God's goodness and faithfulness, and inspires us for what lies ahead.

In the last-but-one reading of this section, Dawn shares her long wait for an elusive man! Her story reminds us that sometimes God will ask us to adjust or even give up our hopes in order to find our true hope in him first.

WHERE ARE YOUR EYES FIXED?

> The Lord upholds all those who fall
> and lifts up all who are bowed down.
> The eyes of all look to you,
> and you give them their food at the proper time.
> You open your hand
> and satisfy the desires of every living thing.
> The Lord is righteous in all his ways
> and loving toward all he has made.
> The Lord is near to all who call on him,
> to all who call on him in truth.
>
> PSALM 145:14–18

The psalmist is expressing how wonderful God's benevolence and care are, and assuring us that our past experience of his provision shows that we can trust him as we wait, now. But these verses also ask us to do something very specific with that sense of trust: 'the eyes of all look to you' (v. 15). We are to focus on God.

Where are you looking while you're waiting? If I stand in the queue with my Christmas shopping, the chances are that I'll keep my eyes fixed on the head of the queue—my destination. I'll be focused on the cashier who, I hope, will move the queue along speedily, the shopper in the queue ahead of me who can't possibly have *that* many relatives to buy presents for, or the young girl fumbling with her purse to count out her last few coins. I just want to reach the end. The bright lights decorating the shop or the tantalizing snatches of conversation I hear around me may temporarily distract me, but mostly I will keep my eyes fixed ahead to where I want to be, in the hope that eventually I will get there.

I'm not so great at doing that as I wait for God's promises to be fulfilled. I often let myself become absorbed by the bright lights, the distractions and the conversation, and throw only a cursory glance in the direction of 'getting there'. I certainly don't keep my eyes fixed on him or rely on him to meet my needs. Instead, I'm looking to everything and everyone but my destination. Yet if I am waiting for him and all he has prepared for me, he should be the one I rely on to meet my needs as I wait, and my eyes should be fixed on him as he draws me ever closer.

It can be a hard thing to keep your eyes 'fixed', can't it? When I visit the optician, she asks me to keep my eyes fixed on a dark dot in the distance while she peers into the depths of each eye with her tiny bright light. It always unnerves me slightly. I wonder what she might spot there! But it's difficult to look straight at that dot and not move or blink. I'd much rather look to see what she is doing, or examine the pictures on the wall, or pull faces at my children, who are usually with me waiting for their turn, highly amused at the state of their staring mother. Yet it's vital that I don't lose my focus if the optician is to do her job effectively.

When we're pressing forward to some goal, it's so much easier to get there if we are fixing our eyes on something or someone ahead. If we fix our eyes on the horizon, the top of the hill we're climbing, the picnic spot we're heading for, or our swimming coach at the end of the pool, we feel drawn onwards, filled with determination, even if we're weary. There's nothing like a light in a window to draw us home, or the sight of a familiar person in the distance—and of course, it is so much easier to 'fix our eyes' on someone, or something, we love.

Perhaps one of the best illustrations of what it means to 'look to' God is a sheepdog, trained to round up and guide a flock at its master's direction. Its eyes will be fixed on the shepherd, watching and listening for the slightest signal to move this way or that, in perfect trust and expectation. The dog's obedience is paramount to the success of the task, and when the job is done there is a reward, companionship and rest. We are called to have this kind of dependence on God our Father, to know him as the sustainer and the provider of all good things, to trust him so surely that we know that we have really lost our focus without him.

Sometimes, of course, we can fix our eyes on the wrong place, become less watchful or in some way preoccupied. Then, whether we admit it or not, we miss God's company and guidance. We may wonder where he is, look all around and feel disappointed that he is not with us as we expected. 'Where were you?' we ask, and he replies, 'Here all the time—right where I said I'd be.' We just hadn't noticed.

A friend of mine tells the story of a day, long before mobile phones, when he had arranged to meet an old schoolfriend in the lobby of a large London hotel. He arrived early and settled himself down next to a pillar to read the newspaper and wait. The minutes went past, and became an hour or more. He could not understand it. His friend was always so reliable. Feeling that he could wait no longer, he decided to leave a note at reception and go to his next appointment. As he walked across the lobby, a familiar voice called out. It was his schoolfriend.

'Where have you been?' exclaimed my friend with a mixture of disbelief and relief.

'Well, right here, where I said I'd be.'

His friend had also spent an hour waiting, his eyes fixed on the door, and had been seated right on the other side of the pillar! On arrival, a few minutes after my friend but still early, he had assumed that he was the first to arrive, and didn't notice a familiar face hidden behind a pillar and a newspaper.

Reflect...

Look back to the last time you had to wait in an everyday situation.

- *Where were your 'eyes fixed' as you waited?*
- *What can you learn from that experience?*
- *When are you most vulnerable to losing your focus on God as you wait?*
- *What could you do to sharpen it?*

Lord Jesus, don't let my sight be dazzled by the bright lights, distracted by the world view, or dimmed by the darkness. Make me aware when you are near. Keep my eyes looking to you.

LIFE-CHANGING CONVERSATIONS

Sometimes waiting enables us to play our part in fulfilling God's wider plan by making the most of opportunities for valuable, even life-changing, conversations. Jesus often had key conversations 'by the way'. If possible, read the full account of this meeting, in John 4:1–42.

Jacob's well was there, and Jesus, tired as he was from the journey, sat down by the well. It was about the sixth hour. When a Samaritan woman came to draw water, Jesus said to her, 'Will you give me a drink?' … The Samaritan woman said to him, 'You are a Jew and I am a Samaritan woman. How can you ask me for a drink?' (For Jews do not associate with Samaritans.) Jesus answered her, 'If you knew who it is that asks you for a drink, you would have asked him and he would have given you living water.'

'Sir,' the woman said, 'you have nothing to draw with and the well is deep. Where can you get this living water? Are you greater than our father Jacob, who gave us the well and drank from it himself, as did his sons and his flocks and herds?'

Jesus answered, 'Everyone who drinks this water will be thirsty again, but whoever drinks the water I give him will never thirst. Indeed, the water I give him will become in him like a spring of water welling up to eternal life.'

The woman said to him, 'Sir, give me this water…'

JOHN 4:6–7, 9–15

It's hard to imagine the midday heat Jesus experienced, if we are shivering in December. Here he is, incredibly human—hot, tired and thirsty—sitting on a wall, waiting for his disciples to return with lunch. A woman approaches him, and his divine insight and knowledge of scripture combine to tell him much about her personal need. This woman, ostracized by her community because of her immoral lifestyle, has perhaps come at this time only because she dare not draw water with others in the cool of the day, although it may have been the tradition for younger women to come at this time, leaving the cooler hours for their elders. Whatever the reason, it is the right time for her.

She ends up in a life-changing conversation as Jesus, starting at a point of his own need, cleverly explores her own needs. He challenges her lifestyle and offers her a new way to live, using the well and its water as an illustration. He is relevant, straightforward and natural in his approach. His moral integrity and directness are uncompromising, and he refuses to be sidetracked by theological argument. With sensitivity, genuine love and compassion, he gives her a vision of a changed and hopeful future. He also gives her dignity, loving her enough to break with the convention that would have prevented their conversation (Jews did not associate freely with Samaritans), and to dispense with 'common sense' (talking freely as a man to an unknown woman), to offer what he knew she needed most.

We might call it 'personal evangelism'; Jesus calls it loving people. I wonder if we recognize that the first proviso for personal evangelism is 'loving enough'. I wonder, too, how often we make the most of casual conversations to share that love. I'm not suggesting that every time we queue in the post office we should prop ourselves on the counter and launch into a sermon, but there may be times when, in the very place and process of waiting, we are able to engage with others and offer Jesus as a way of meeting their needs.

When I was a student, I got into the habit of praying about the long train journeys home and those I might meet and talk with as I waited for trains to arrive and journeys to pass. God often gave me the points of contact from which to talk in a natural way about my faith, with Christians and non-Christians alike. The same has been true of time spent waiting at the hospital during my years of cancer treatment and follow-up appointments. I have often found myself alongside those who are anxious or afraid. Their vulnerability means that they are especially open to a friendly chat, my care, and often my offers to pray for or even with them.

God gives us a remarkable privilege when he leads his needy and hurting children into our paths, even as we wait. It's true that people want to know we care, before they care about what we know. Nothing will draw people to Jesus more than the knowledge that he, and we, genuinely care about them.

Another friend of mine learnt the lesson of Jesus' 'waiting' conversation and put it into practice. One year, at Christmas, she found herself standing next to a man and his wife in a supermarket checkout queue. The lines were long and the trolleys piled high. Grinning at each other, they began to chat. Then, acknowledging the queues and the trolleys, the man gestured at both and asked, 'What's all this Christmas lark for, then?' My friend, deciding that she could not miss an opportunity to 'love enough', took a deep breath and began: 'Well, actually…' She shared simply why Christmas and the gift of Jesus were important to her and to her family. By the time they had reached the end of the queue, she had invited the man and his family for mince pies at a church Christmas social event. As far as I understand, he and his wife joined an Alpha course in the new year, and became Christians shortly afterwards. They doubtless viewed their wait in a supermarket queue in very different terms from then on!

We might not always find that our waiting conversations have such happy and productive endings—but perhaps we should hope for them more often.

Reflect…

Where do you wait regularly and so fall into conversation with those waiting alongside you? How might you realistically begin to develop those 'waiting words' into 'life-changing words'? Ask God to make those words relevant, loving—and bold.

Father God, wherever I wait for time to pass today, in a queue, a waiting-room, a train, bus or taxi, don't allow an opportunity to pass with the time. Help me to 'love enough' to break the silence. Give me words that will transform the minutes through which I wait—and maybe even transform a life.

TIME OUT

Trust in the Lord and do good;
dwell in the land and enjoy safe pasture.
Delight yourself in the Lord
and he will give you the desires of your heart.
Commit your way to the Lord;
trust in him and he will do this:
He will make your righteousness shine like the dawn,
the justice of your cause like the noonday sun.
Be still before the Lord and wait patiently for him;
do not fret when men succeed in their ways,
when they carry out their wicked schemes.
Refrain from anger and turn from wrath;
do not fret—it leads only to evil.
For evil men will be cut off,
but those who hope in the Lord will inherit the land.

PSALM 37:3–9

If anyone was qualified to write such words of wisdom and assurance in the Lord, it was David. They are woven into a recurring theme in which he parallels the apparent prosperity of the wicked with the eternal security of the righteous, and even if we put that parallel aside, his rules for living are simple, clear and powerful.

Trust in the Lord... delight in him... don't worry or get angry... hope in him and he'll reward you.

'If only it were so easy!' we cry. Yet there at the heart of the psalm lies the key to the kind of trust and assurance David advocates: 'Be still before the Lord and wait patiently for him' (v. 7). In other words, we're not to jump up and down telling God what we think he should do, impatiently waiting for him to get a move on and passing him frequent reminder notes. Instead, we should take time out in stillness. We need to look to God in trust and dependence, consider his perspective and his timing, and seek his counsel—to 'be still before the Lord'.

Does that mean we stop in our tracks? As we develop our waiting skills, do we sit down on the job, empty our minds and abandon ourselves in an ignorant haze to whatever God has planned for us? Should we let ourselves be swept along with a beatific smile etched on our faces? Not if we look at the verses that surround those quoted in today's reading.

There is a sense of everyday busyness within them, of living life to the full in righteousness and truth. Here is a picture of God's people laughing, working the land and enjoying the fruits of labour despite the actions of wicked men, and always trusting in the provision, protection and goodness of God. They are getting on with life. But in the midst of the busyness of getting on with life, we also need to take time out to draw on his wisdom, as we wait for him and on him.

Whenever I am in a city and find myself being sucked into its hustle and bustle, I look for a church building where I can step out of the busy street and into an oasis of calm to regain something of God's perspective on my day. Often I will walk through huge doors and hear them close heavily behind me, sealing off the sound outside. Almost immediately I will look up and acknowledge what appears to be a different world—a world of quiet, where time itself seems to be standing still; a place that seems quite unperturbed by the worries of the world, and one that towers quite literally above and beyond its cares.

To stand on the threshold of such a place reminds me of the constant nature of God. Just as the church building waits to offer a space for those who want to take time out, God waits for me. So I will sit for a while, maybe only a few minutes, and turn my mind more fully towards him. I will offer him the day, the meeting ahead, the work I'm doing, the concerns of others; or I will just sit in awe at the place, at the gifts of craftsmanship he gave to those who laboured on the building, at the sweep of an arch or the kaleidoscope of coloured light that filters through a window—and eventually I feel awe at God himself. When he has met with me, as I have waited in the stillness, I will rejoin that busy world outside. God always rewards those 'time out' moments, although not always in the way I expect and not always immediately. Sometimes I have left the grandest cathedral feeling disappointed, almost frustrated, thinking, 'What was the point of that? Did God meet with me?' Only later will I hear or see something, or listen to a word somebody speaks, at some point in the rest of that busy day, and realize that he did indeed meet with me. It is only once I am back in the busyness that I recognize his voice.

I am reminded too that while the vastness and beauty of a building, with its cool and quiet, might help me focus, the place where I really find God, wherever I might be, is in the quiet of my heart. My 'cathedral' may be the edge of a forest, on a motorway flyover, in an ordinary kitchen, or in the corner of an office. I just have to find that space in my heart. God will be there to meet me.

---

reflect...

Drop thy still dews of quietness,
till all our strivings cease.
Take from our souls the strain and stress
and let our ordered lives confess
the beauty of thy peace,
the beauty of thy peace.
JOHN GREENLEAF WHITTIER (1807–92)

Lord, it is often easier said than done. Teach me to wait in patience and stillness.

READING BETWEEN THE LINES

Tychicus will tell you all the news about me. He is a dear brother, a faithful minister and fellow servant in the Lord. I am sending him to you for the express purpose that you may know about our circumstances and that he may encourage your hearts. He is coming with Onesimus, our faithful and dear brother, who is one of you. They will tell you everything that is happening here. My fellow prisoner Aristarchus sends you his greetings, as does Mark, the cousin of Barnabas. (You have received instructions about him; if he comes to you, welcome him.) Jesus, who is called Justus, also sends greetings. These are the only Jews among my fellow workers for the kingdom of God, and they have proved a comfort to me. Epaphras, who is one of you and a servant of Jesus Christ, sends greetings. He is always wrestling in prayer for you, that you may stand firm in all the will of God, mature and fully assured. I vouch for him that he is working hard for you and for those at Laodicea and Hierapolis. Our dear friend Luke, the doctor, and Demus send greetings. Give my greetings to the brothers at Laodicea, and to Nympha and the church in her house.

After this letter has been read to you, see that it is also read in the church of the Laodiceans and that you in turn read the letter from Laodicea. Tell Archippus: 'See to it that you complete the work you have received in the Lord.'

I, Paul, write this greeting in my own hand. Remember my chains. Grace be with you.

COLOSSIANS 4:7–18

About this time of year, as the Christmas cards start arriving, so do the 'round robin' Christmas letters, those newsy missives detailing the lives and loves of family and friends worldwide. I have to admit, shamefully, that until this year I had a certain dread of this flood of epistles. I rarely seemed to find time to read more than the first one or two, and some of them made me, my children's educational achievements and hobbies and our family holiday destinations seem very dull indeed. I didn't want to know that Clare had ten A*s at GCSE after just a year's study and David, aged three, had attained Grade 8 at piano—especially when I had been nagging my daughter even to glance at her homework and my son had given up the recorder after the first lesson in fits of breathy giggles. Neither did I want to hear about the 'glorious fortnight in the Maldives' when we'd suffered a rainy week in Derbyshire—beautiful though it is—during a week of significant football matches with all their attendant complications ('But we can't go out—there's a match on!').

This year, however, I found myself severely rebuked as I opened my first 'family letter', after an incidental conversation with an elderly friend. She has no family, although she has a multitude of friends, and she shared with me just how much joy such letters bring her. She told me, quite without self-pity and with some excitement, that they gave her a glimpse of everyday family life that she has never known. Despite her limited experience of its ups and downs, she said, wisely, 'But of course, you have to read between the lines, don't you? The real life is hidden in the insignificant detail.' She's right. No family life is perfect. It's the details of to-ing and fro-ing, recognizable names and 'can't help but mention' memories that are important, not the big moments and high achievements.

It's the same in these verses from Colossians. At first glance we may see little of note in Paul's final words. Certainly there is little direct teaching, but these wonderful greetings, which seem to include anyone and everyone, are the everyday human story of Paul's ministry. We can recognize some names we know well and read others we know hardly at all. We recognize Luke, whose compassionate account of Jesus' ministry we read in the Gospel that bears his name, and Onesimus, whose 'escape' and conversion Paul writes about in his letter to Onesimus' former master, Philemon. Then there are the men and women who lead the church, the prayer group leaders, the doers and the fellow workers. Paul includes and values them all. This is more than a letter warning about false teaching and guidance in the practicalities of church life. This last chapter shows us that it's a newsy one, too. Within these greetings we glimpse comings and goings, friendly chatter and welcome back-slapping, clear evidence of looking out for one another, the sharing of meals and real community.

The early Church needed not just Paul, but one another. Paul knew that their unity was essential to their survival and growth, and he encouraged them to care for each other in order to maintain it. We can pick out from the greetings some of the elements of community life that are as vital now as they were in the early Church: 'encourage', 'telling', 'fellow workers', 'comfort', 'prayer', 'working hard'. It's not just in the heroic acts or great spiritual moments that we find the kind of love and community God desires, but in the small, selfless acts and gifts of time and energy. It fills the days when we choose just to be with someone who needs our company, help to share their load or take a moment to send a card or a word of encouragement to one for whom it will make more difference than we might ever know. That's real loving and living community. This kind of living is also the way in which we can share the love of God with those who don't yet know him. Just by being there and waiting with them, and by attending to the small detail of their lives.

When I was in hospital recovering from a stem cell transplant as part of my cancer treatment, a friend who is a night nurse at a hospice a few miles away would call in to my isolation room on the ward every morning on her way home. It was always very early, but she scrubbed up and gowned up and, however tired she was feeling, would sit with me until the hospital day began and then go home to sleep. Sometimes we would chat; other times I would be asleep or feeling too ill to say very much. Whatever the situation, Jacqui would simply sit with me and wait for the day to begin. Those hours would often otherwise have been lonely. Building community and loving each other does involve the hustle and bustle of meeting and greeting and serving one another. Sometimes, however, it involves no more than just waiting together.

Reflect...

Ask yourself: Who might I 'sit and wait' with today?

Father God, as I learn the art of waiting, teach me to build real community in the small detail of life. Make me sensitive to the light and shade of the experience of others. May I be ready to rejoice in their sunshine, and stand beside them in the shadows.

MIND YOUR 'P'S—
BUT ESPECIALLY YOUR 'Q'S

That day David first committed to Asaph and his associates this psalm of thanks to the Lord:

> Give thanks to the Lord, call on his name;
> make known among the nations what he has done.
> Sing to him, sing praise to him;
> tell of all his wonderful acts.
> Glory in his holy name;
> let the hearts of those who seek the Lord rejoice.
> Look to the Lord and his strength;
> seek his face always.
> Remember the wonders he has done,
> his miracles, and the judgment he pronounced,
> O descendants of Israel his servant,
> O sons of Jacob, his chosen ones.
>
> 1 CHRONICLES 16:7–13

The ark of the covenant has been brought to Jerusalem, so King David gives thanks—and how! This was a celebration to top all celebrations. There had been processions, sacrifices and fellowship offerings, feasting, singing and dancing—and here, David has written something special for the occasion as a praise finale.

This psalm is similar to a number of other psalms written by David, which encapsulate the true heart of thanksgiving before God. It contains a model we could well use in times of waiting in our daily lives.

'*Give thanks*': There is so much that God has done for us—his provision for our daily needs, his grace, the gift of his Son, the hope of our future with him...

'*Make known*': Sharing the good news of Jesus with those who don't yet know him as Lord can also be an act of thanksgiving in itself.

'*Sing*': The heart of our worship is thanksgiving, so we too should sing, whether we really do 'make a joyful noise' or not.

'*Tell*': We can encourage each other in our Christian lives and give thanks to God at the same time by sharing all he has done for us with one another.

'*Glory in his name*': We can both acknowledge the power and authority that exist in the very name of Jesus as Lord and appreciate the beauty of that name we love in thanksgiving.

'*Seek him*': He longs to be found by us, and if we seek him 'he will be found' (2 Chronicles 15:2).

'*Look to him*': If he is our focus, we cannot lose our bearings, and we cannot fail to be thankful for his direction.

'*Remember what he has done*': Simply looking back over our lives and recognizing his hand on the events that have shaped them and the lives of others leads us to greater thankfulness. It is wonderful to nurture a thankful heart. Thankfulness lifts our whole being. It is infectious, encouraging, and never fails to make us smile.

We can begin by asking God to give us a spirit of thankfulness, a seed that will grow—but often the hard groundwork will be down to us. We may have to discipline ourselves consciously to be thankful, day by day. We will water the seed of thankfulness as we pray, in recognition of God's goodness and in all circumstances. It may be a childlike practice, but it's not a bad one—to 'count your blessings'.

I can be a bit of a moaner sometimes. It's mostly light-hearted moaning, but my long-suffering husband sometimes says I wouldn't be happy if I didn't have something to moan about. That's not a great reputation to have, even with a husband who miraculously loves me anyway, so I consciously try to do something about it. If I hear myself moan or criticize, I automatically try to follow with at least two positive points. Just the act of doing that lifts my heart, and before I go to sleep at night I try to think of six things in the day to be thankful for. Sometimes it's a struggle, and sometimes I'll be asleep before I've reached number four, but it's not a bad way to fall asleep, and I know God honours my attempts.

The spirit of thankfulness was perfectly illustrated in a church service one Christmas Eve. The celebration was especially designed for the children—an opportunity to share the nativity story and focus on the real meaning of Christmas before the distractions of the big day began. The church was decorated with bright lights, a tree and a life-size crib scene. Hours of preparation had gone into making everything perfect. The children sang, and the nativity story was flawlessly acted out. Then, towards the end of the service, we prepared to pray together. Several of the children had been heavily rehearsed to read prayers of intercession. There was a long prayer about the needs of those in the local hospital and nearby residential homes, and another for those who would be alone at Christmas.

Finally, a very tiny child, who had been given the honoured task of saying a 'thank you' prayer, stepped forward. She had obviously been briefed beforehand and knew that she would be saying thank you to Jesus. As she was too young to read, her mum was poised at the bottom of the stage, ready to whisper the lines for her to follow word by word. Standing on the stage, waiting for her moment, she was suddenly overcome by the sight of the bright lights, the decorations, her assorted doting grandparents, aunts and uncles and the promise of Christmas. Instead of following her mother's words, she turned to the audience, momentarily flung her arms in the air and then clasped her hands tightly together in front of her chest as if to squeeze out all her delight. With a sudden leap in the air she piped at the top of her voice, 'Oh! Thank you! Thank you! Lovely Christmas Jesus!' It was all that was needed. The congregation burst into applause.

Reflect...

Read Psalm 100, as a prayer:

> *Shout for joy to the Lord, all the earth.*
> *Worship the Lord with gladness;*
> *come before him with joyful songs.*
> *Know that the Lord is God.*
> *It is he who made us, and we are his;*
> *we are his people, the sheep of his pasture.*
> *Enter his gates with thanksgiving*
> *and his courts with praise;*
> *give thanks to him and praise his name.*
> *For the Lord is good and his love endures for ever;*
> *his faithfulness continues through all generations.*

Now allow yourself to be caught up in the excitement of thankfulness!

DAWN: WAITING FOR MIKE

> Those who sow in tears
> will reap with songs of joy.
> Those who go out weeping,
> carrying seed to sow,
> will return with songs of joy,
> carrying sheaves with them.
>
> PSALM 126:5–6

Dawn is a trainer and evangelist with Open Air Campaigners, a national organization that shares the good news of Jesus on the street, in schools and through special church-based celebrations. Dawn was single until her marriage to Mike in 2001, at the age of 44. This is her story of a long wait.

'You have it all worked out, don't you? When you are young and off to college, you just know that you will meet someone special and get married. Actually, my plan was to get married at the age of 25, as I couldn't imagine myself settling down and being a responsible grown-up before that. So off I went to college in the sure and certain hope that the right guy was just around the corner.

'The crop of weddings that flourished in the summer after our final year was second to none. Only, somehow, mine didn't seem to be among them. Of course I had the usual range of attractions to different guys in the Christian Union and really good friendships with some of them, but never anything more. I fantasized, I agonized, I probably even drooled, but nothing ever happened. Waiting was a frustrating experience. Life went on and the working schedule of being a house-mistress in girls' boarding schools did nothing for my love life.

'In case you get the idea that I was placidly accepting the situation, I ought to put you right. I was not! I had very long conversations—no, be honest, arguments—with God about the matter. "Lord, you must have someone for me somewhere. I really need a man! I need to be loved and cared for."

'Then came a light on the horizon: I went off to Bible college. Of course I would find a man there! I didn't, though—not even a possibility. They were all too young, too old, or already attached, so at the end of another two years I was still waiting, ever more impatiently, for God to find me a life partner.

'After three years working in a church, I moved to Plymouth to become an evangelist, 29 years old, still single and still wishing I wasn't. There were times when I was happy with life and happy to say to the Lord, "If you want me to stay single, then that's fine by me." At other times I cried because I so wanted to be held and loved. I felt the loneliness of my single life the most whenever anything went wrong, when the pressure of the job became too great or, worst of all, when I found myself in conferences with seminars entitled "How to keep your marriage going in ministry" (yuck).

'There was one man, however, I was sure the Lord had in mind for us to be together. I have never been more certain of anything in my life. But he just didn't see it like that. That kind of slap in the face is tough when you are a lovesick teenager but infinitely more so when you are a 30-something reluctant single. I was still on the rollercoaster ride of being content and then screaming at God, "Why am I still single? Why am I still waiting?"

'Contentment finally came (but still no husband!) eight years ago. God said, "You have to give up that hope." You see, all the while I hoped for a man, I obviously wasn't content with what God had given me. It was the hardest battle I have ever fought. I wept and mourned. I felt like Jephthah's daughter, who, on hearing of her imminent demise, asked for time to "weep with my friends, because

I will never marry" (Judges 11:37). It wasn't that God was saying I would never marry (although, at 37, I had to admit it was a long shot) but that I must stop hoping for it, which meant living as if I never would.

'I once had a bookmark that said, "If you commit yourself to your cross, the need will lose its bitterness." It's true! I was finally content. I had given up all hope of marriage, husband and children and was content just to be me. I would have called myself a committed single—not necessarily called to permanent singleness, but if this was the place that God had for me at the moment, I was committed to it and happy with it. So the waiting was over. There was no more hope for a man, so there was no more waiting.

'Then along came Mike! We had known each other for years and he was recently widowed. Our friendship blossomed. Getting married was the hardest decision I have ever had to make. I was, at last, happy and contented as a single woman, and along came a man to cause havoc and upset my ordered existence. Emotionally I was a teenager again, with the highs and lows of being in love—if ever I could work out what that meant. However, I finally did it, for better or worse, richer or poorer and all the rest, in March 2002, at the ripe old age of 44. I love being married now, although it has taken a lot of getting used to. There are still times when I look back to being single with just a touch of wistfulness; and as for children, well I have to admit it's a long shot at my age, but there's one thing I have done—I've learnt to wait and see!'

Reflect...

Meditate on the Bible verses at the start of today's reading, and then turn them into a prayer of praise.

KEEP YOUR EYES OPEN

The Lord is my light and my salvation—
whom shall I fear?
The Lord is the stronghold of my life—
of whom shall I be afraid? ...
One thing I ask of the Lord,
this is what I seek:
that I may dwell in the house of the Lord
all the days of my life,
to gaze upon the beauty of the Lord
and to seek him in his temple.
For in the day of trouble
he will keep me safe in his dwelling;
he will hide me in the shadow of his tabernacle
and set me high upon a rock...
I am still confident of this:
I will see the goodness of the Lord
in the land of the living.
Wait for the Lord;
be strong and take heart
and wait for the Lord.

PSALM 27:1, 4–5, 13–14

While we may view our times of waiting as wasted time, God
certainly doesn't. He will often teach us more in the waiting time
than through the very thing we are waiting for. This week of readings
has shown us that far from nodding off in a cosy 'waiting place', we
should be alert and on the lookout for what God is asking us to do

while we wait. More importantly, we should be on the lookout for God himself, for he will certainly want to share our waiting space. In order not to miss him, we may need to learn to really look at him, so that we can recognize him when he approaches and hear his voice when he speaks.

My daughter is (and excuse me while I 'blow her trumpet') something of an accomplished artist. To encourage her in this interest, we asked a friend who is a professional artist to spend time with her, so that she could make the most of her gifts. Anita worked with Lois once a week, explaining colour, tone and perspective, and helping her to develop her skills. Very early on she emphasized the need for Lois to look carefully at what she wanted to draw. 'Look,' she would say. '*Really* look at your subject, and keep looking as you draw. Lose yourself in what you see.'

Developing the skills of an artist depends on good observation. Learning the art of waiting is no exception. We need to learn to look, really look to God—with trust, dependence and hope. What's more, we will find it much easier to wait if we can lose ourselves in what we see. Making sure he is our focus as we wait means that we can never be disappointed. Our hope in him is eternal, timeless, not time-limited. It will move us on in trust and solid dependence in the one who never lets us down, turns up late or forgets an appointment.

Ask yourself: How can I be sure that God himself, and his plan, is my focus? We may need to begin by considering whether we really are focusing on God as he would have us see him, or simply on the familiar, portable, adaptable God we've always taken for granted. Many of us may have formed an idea of God in our childhood that sticks. A childlike view of God is not necessarily a bad thing, but often, while we mature, our image of God doesn't. We limit his impact on our lives because the picture we prefer to carry around with us is one that doesn't do him justice. It is too simplistic. Like a picture drawn by a child, it may be charming but it lacks depth, the evidence of experience and the perspective of maturity. We may even find that we have become too comfortable with that simple picture, and that we resist more depth and detail in our knowledge of God, clinging to that childlike image. He could be simply asking us to 'grow up' in the way we see him, because he knows that we will never really recognize him and know him if we don't. Just as Lois was taught to 'really look' to produce a true and life-like image, so we need to 'really look' at God to ensure that our knowledge of him is not only accurate, but life-like, for we need to get to know the true God.

We can develop our knowledge of him by spending more time to 'gaze upon the beauty of the Lord and to seek him in his temple' (v. 4). That might involve silent contemplation, or a walk in a stunning landscape, literally gazing on all he has made and in which his creativity and joy can be found.

To seek God, we might commit ourselves to a biblical exploration of who God is and what he is really like. A thematic Bible can help us explore the richness, the love and the life-giving attributes of God's character. Exploring one attribute a month—his wisdom or his faithfulness, for example—can help us draw a more detailed and tender picture of our marvellous God. It can also transform our worship as we begin to see him, and so worship him, as he really is.

As our picture of God gains depth and detail, we might also gain a fresh perspective on our times of waiting. Spending time with him, waiting for him and sharing his perspective on our lives—and his wider plan—may alter our view of much more than just our current situation. It may even give us a privileged glimpse of the masterplan of our life that he holds in his hands. But we need to take time to do that.

Reflect...

Ask yourself: When could I take time out over the holiday period ahead to gaze on God and seek him? And how might those times help me wait for him?

Amazing, unfathomable God, one day I will see you in your glory as you really are. But for now, help me find that glory reflected in the detail of my days: in love given and received, in the artistry of your creation, in the small miracles of birth and life. As I trace those glorious details, teach me to gaze and wonder.

✛

PATIENCE BECOMES HOPE

GALLERY: 'THE TIMEPIECE'

An old clock stands before you at eye level on a plinth. It is made of wood and leather, glass and copper, silver and brass. It has no date-mark, yet somehow its great age is apparent in every detail, as if it was crafted almost before time. Its face is protected by flawless glass; its hood is burnished copper, gleaming under the gallery lights. Its case is made of a rare wood, so highly polished to a perfect finish that it reflects everything around it, but there is also great security and strength in the case that so secretly hides the mechanism within.

Its cogs and wheels have been precisely measured, honed and calibrated so that not a second is lost. There are hundreds if not thousands of parts, all working to time. Large cogs and tiny spindles and wheels, threads of copper wire like hair, screws and bolts so minute that they could be lost in the edge of a fingernail.

At the base of the clock is a revolving movement. Inside it, the figure of a tiny brass man is balanced on a disc. He is in a hurry, and as he runs he is looking at what appears to be another timepiece, pulled from a pocket or bag somewhere on his person, perhaps from a breast-pocket like the white rabbit's in *Alice in Wonderland*. His cheeks are puffed out and his legs are posed to run as he silently whirs round and round. How ridiculous he looks from on high—a comical picture!

The clock's outer casing carries a brass plate delicately etched with a bigger picture. Sun, moon, stars and clouds appear to dance around one another. They dwarf the tiny figure below, making him insignificant, yet in some way seeming to offer him protection.

The clock is a harmony of balance and grace, art and science, past and present. Turning hour by hour since the first cog was set in motion, it is still keeping perfect time. You sense that it is so well balanced and so well maintained with love and painstaking care that it will never lose time. It will never gallop too fast into the future, never slow down into the past, never stop or refuse to strike the hour, swing its pendulum out of rhythm or chime out of spite.

The movements are so small, so delicate, so precisely aligned that as seconds turn to a minute, hardly any change is discerned, and as you hold your breath all you hear is a faint tick. It is a tick that flicks not a moment too soon or a moment too late, hardly discernible but perfectly timed.

As you walk around the clock, the light plays on the polished wooden case and the brass plate. It falls on to the figure on his spinning disc and projects tiny beams and flickers of reflected light across the room and against the gallery wall like a light-show.

The label shows no date of acquisition or country of origin—just the words, 'This is a Masterpiece'.

INTRODUCTION

I wonder if you are somewhat distracted today by thoughts of the packing and preparation involved in going away for Christmas. My husband and I always find it amusing that we have very different approaches to the start of a holiday or a trip to visit friends or family. I will plan and pack for days beforehand, writing lists, checking them, getting the children organized in packing their own bags, and packing both mine and my husband's. I will water plants, check the garden, write notes for the neighbours, cancel the paper and clear the fridge, finally placing all the bags and equipment in the hall ready to go in the car. I leave just a few last-minute jobs to do while the boot is filled with the luggage. By this time, the children will be ready and aching to go. They will make their last trip to the bathroom, remember something they really must have, and settle themselves either in the car or on the wall outside the house—and wait for their dad. And I will wait with them.

And we will wait… and wait.

Then begins the comedy show of watching Dad run up and down the stairs, emerging from the front door every few minutes with a 'Have you got…?'

'Yes.'

Then, 'Did you pack…?'

'Three pairs.'

'Have you remembered…?'

'Of course.'

Next, there will be a leisurely selection of music to play in the car (which will invariably be in the car already), a search for the newspaper (which will usually be left behind on the kitchen table anyway), and finally, 'Glasses, where did I put my glasses?'

The children joke that the three of us could go for a short holiday while Dad gets ready to drive off on this one. Any thoughts of leaving at the crack of dawn to make the most of every day disappeared from my mind years ago. We are lucky if we leave by lunch-time.

This is waiting of the most frustrating kind. It's a time I should use to take stock, check the packing, plan the journey ahead, even pop round and say hello to the neighbours. I could contemplate the trees, the sky, even my bitten fingernails. But of course I don't. I look at my watch. God is still teaching me to be patient!

If waiting is an art, patience is its most essential skill. When God asks us to wait patiently, and then to wait again, it is never an easy request to understand. He might be offering us the opportunity to take stock or gain strength before we move on. Perhaps we need to learn or relearn something we missed, or check some details for our spiritual journey, getting our bearings before pushing on ahead. He may long for us to set our dreams before him rather than settle for 'good enough', or he may simply want us to enjoy basking in the wonder of his glory.

Just occasionally we may think we are waiting for him—when, in fact, he is waiting for us.

THE PLANE NOW BOARDING...

Because of the Lord's great love we are not consumed,
for his compassions never fail.
They are new every morning;
great is your faithfulness.
I say to myself, 'The Lord is my portion;
therefore I will wait for him.'
The Lord is good to those whose hope is in him;
it is good to wait quietly
for the salvation of the Lord.

LAMENTATIONS 3:22–26

This beautiful passage appears in the middle of a heart-wrenching lament about the state of the desolate city of Jerusalem. It is as if the writer (probably Jeremiah) has raised his head from his composition of general downheartedness to remind himself that, despite it all, God is faithful. The whole of this chapter focuses on God as the Lord of hope, faithfulness, compassion, love and salvation—despite what was happening all around. Sometimes, even amid a desolate or bewildering time of waiting, we need to hold on to the truth of these words. They rise above the uncertainty of life, the longing for fulfilment, and remind us to place our trust in the all-knowing God.

We often feel temporarily overlooked or neglected in our day-to-day lives. Bureaucracy, busyness and red tape frequently leave us wondering if we have been reduced to little more than a name and number on a sheet in the depths of a file. If we're confined to a waiting-room of some description, perhaps in a hospital, an impersonal public building or a railway station, it can be worse. We can't go anywhere for fear of missing our turn or our train, or running the risk of not being in the right place when we're wanted. We're ready to go, but we have to wait to be called.

Occasionally, we might feel as if our spiritual lives mirror those practical everyday situations. Sometimes God may be telling us that it's time to go, but for some reason we've missed our call. It could be that we're not hearing—or don't want to hear. Perhaps we have become too comfortable in our waiting place. Our spiritual muscles may have stiffened into a permanent waiting posture, head down, focus lost.

Mehran Karimi Nasseri, an Iranian exile, landed at Charles de Gaulle airport in Paris in 1988. At the time of writing, he is still there. Having arrived without the correct papers, French authorities let him stay on while waiting for the missing documentation, as long as he remained in the confines of the airport. When his papers finally arrived—seven years later—he was free to go. But he stayed where he was, living in the departure lounge, washing in the public washrooms. It's the life he knows best. Paranoia has led him to believe that he will be arrested if he leaves the airport. He reads widely, but never goes outside. The last time he dared was to watch the eclipse in 1999.

He has made friends with the airport staff, he was allowed to keep 'his' bench to sleep on when the rest were removed for improvements, airport personnel have campaigned for him to be allowed to stay, and they regularly help him with food tokens and gifts. Having become something of a celebrity, it is not unusual for him to sign autographs for waiting passengers.

Nassari has endured a long legal immigration battle in Belgium, France and the UK as a result of misplaced papers, mistaken advice and misunderstandings. He is undoubtedly confused, and possibly ill. There seems to be no one who can really help him, and he feels he can do little more except continue his wait. Lawyers say he will probably end his days at the airport, and it is quite likely that he will literally die waiting.[6]

His story brings to mind the invalid at the pool of Bethesda who had been waiting 38 years for healing. Jesus asked him, 'Do you want to get well?' but the man avoided the question by pointing to others rather than acknowledging his own responsibility (John 5:1–15). Similarly, in Samuel Beckett's play Waiting for Godot, two characters, Vladimir and Estragon, wait in the same place, day after day, for 'Godot' to arrive for some vaguely prearranged meeting. Neither character really knows what, or even whom, to expect, but their waiting is never over, and begins again at the start of each day. Waiting has become life, and life has become waiting.

We can be very much like Nassari, the man at the pool, Vladimir and Estragon in our spiritual lives, waiting in the place where we feel safe and comfortable spiritually, while God is telling us to leave. God may want us to be bold and fly to new destinations where our spiritual growth and development can benefit from new climes, sights and sounds. We may, in a strange way, prefer the barrenness of a spiritually empty place, may even enjoy being where others are leaving and arriving, passing through and visiting new and exciting places. But we remain fearful of what might be beyond the open door, imprisoning ourselves to stay in a place where our waiting might never be over.

When God calls us to leave our waiting place, and we feel unprepared, we may need to ask for courage to take that first step towards the door, because one step is all it takes to get moving. If we don't, we risk trapping ourselves in our own spiritual airport departure lounge.

Reflect...

Is there anything that is keeping you in your own 'spiritual departure lounge'? What might you need to do to gain your 'boarding pass' and take off? Ask God to give you the courage to walk towards—and through—the gate.

Lord, sometimes I long for the wait to end. But then, when you say it's time to leave, I drag my feet. I will not leave my spiritual departure lounge. I develop a fear of flying where you would have me soar. Give me the courage to end my wait, take off, and begin to live.

A LONG WAIT FOR THE LIGHT

Nevertheless, there will be no more gloom for those who were in distress. In the past he humbled the land of Zebulun and the land of Naphtali, but in the future he will honour Galilee of the Gentiles, by the way of the sea, along the Jordan—

> The people walking in darkness
> have seen a great light;
> on those living in the land of the shadow of death
> a light has dawned.
> You have enlarged their nation
> and increased their joy;
> they rejoice before you
> as people rejoice at the harvest,
> as men rejoice
> when dividing the plunder.
> For as in the day of Midian's defeat,
> you have shattered
> the yoke that burdens them,
> the bar across their shoulders,
> the rod of their oppressor.
> Every warrior's boot used in battle
> and every garment rolled in blood
> will be destined for burning,
> will be fuel for the fire.
> For unto us a child is born,
> unto us a son is given,
> and the government will be on his shoulders.

And he will be called
Wonderful Counsellor, Mighty God
Everlasting Father, Prince of Peace.
Of the increase of his government and peace
there will be no end.
He will reign on David's throne
and over his kingdom,
establishing and upholding it
with justice and righteousness
from that time on and for ever.
The zeal of the Lord Almighty
will accomplish this.

ISAIAH 9:1–7

These words from Isaiah 9 are my favourite Advent reading. They also form the official start to my personal Christmas celebrations. Each year on Christmas Eve I listen to the service of Nine Lessons and Carols from King's College, Cambridge, on the radio, and when these words are read I am generally in the midst of preparing the vegetables for the Christmas lunch we'll share the following day. In fact, it has become such a habit that I can tell how far behind I am with the preparations by whether I'm peeling carrots or making pastry or haven't got as far as either!

In the midst of all the domestic humdrum and final hours of waiting for 'the day', these words remind me of just how long Israel had to wait for the words of Isaiah's prophecy to be fulfilled. The promises God made to his people didn't come to fruition for many lifetimes, yet they were fulfilled, after a long wait, in Jesus. Notice how many times the words 'will', 'he will' or 'will be' appear. Perhaps they were meant to be read with an emphasis that would underline the certainty of God's word and intention across the years to come. Isaiah couldn't have known that his small part in the bigger picture would take so long to complete. God was drawing the pencil outline that would be filled in over succeeding generations. Isaiah had to be content with a tantalizing sketch of what was to come.

A proverb says that 'it is better to plant the seed of a great tree than to sit under the shade of its branches'. Sometimes we will achieve more, leave greater things behind, and have greater plans fulfilled, if we can be content with sowing a seed rather than being around for the harvest. We may need to acknowledge that we will not receive what we are waiting for in our lifetime, but God still hears our longings and has them in hand. He may have planned even better things for us than we could dream.

I once attended a service of thanksgiving for the life of a clergyman I knew, whom I'll call James. He had been involved in the youth and student ministry at the church I attended and had been a great influence on my own spiritual life. He was a lovely man— quiet and reflective, with a rare insight into the gifts of others and a unique way of encouraging them to dream big dreams and live them out. The church was packed for the service and, as is often the case, James' family had asked a number of people to say a few words about him during the service. As each person spoke, a familiar theme emerged. One young man shared how James had encouraged him to stick to his musical studies as a reluctant teenager. He told the congregation that he was just finishing at music college, having passed his exams with distinction, and was now on the threshold of a promising professional career. A woman from the church spoke of how James had encouraged her to set up a day nursery, which had become a lifeline for parents in her community and had given her a focus and a purpose after the tragic early death of her own husband.

Everyone I talked with afterwards had been encouraged in some way by James to 'go with their gifts', sometimes with amazing results. When I spoke to his widow a few weeks later, she told me how wonderful the occasion had been. She explained that James had often felt that he hadn't achieved anything spectacular in his ministry. They had never served as a couple in the kind of parishes he had dreamt of as a young curate, and never seemed to be at the 'cutting edge' of things. But now she had realized (and she had a hunch that James had too) that he had achieved so much more by encouraging others to fulfil their gifts, hopes and dreams, and that his life's work, albeit cut tragically short, had created 'a ripple in the pool' effect. Had he served in those 'cutting edge' parishes, he would probably never have had the time to invest in those whose gifts he encouraged with such remarkable results. In a sense, James had had to wait beyond his lifetime to see the fruits of his labours and the effect of his very special gift of encouragement.

I have always loved music. As a child I longed to play the piano but there were four children in the family and the money for lessons —let alone a piano—could not be found. I couldn't understand my schoolfriend, who was lucky enough (in my opinion) to have lessons, but was reluctant to practise! In later years, I grew to love the sound of the cello, and now somewhat envy a friend of my husband, who began to learn to play in his 40th year. But I know that learning either instrument at this point in my busy life is still not practical. I will have to wait. I light-heartedly shared this longing with a wise Christian friend the other day, and she suggested I pray about it from another perspective. She said that even if I can't learn now, who's to say that someday, in a new earth or in heaven, it might not be possible for me to learn both the piano and the cello. My simple dream may not be fulfilled in my earthly lifetime, but I think God understands that longing and will bless it, however long I have to wait, and that one day there'll be no stopping me!

Reflect...

Do you have a longing in your family life, work or ministry that you are waiting for God to fulfil—or something you ache to see ended? Bring it to him now in prayer.

Father God, we do not always fully recognize the picture you outline in our lives. You may not choose to complete it until much later, or you may take years to fill in its shape with the colours of your choosing. We may be confused by a design half completed, or wait until eternity to see it from the artist's viewpoint. Give us the patience to allow you to finish what promises to be a masterpiece, for we know, Lord, that you 'will accomplish this'.

MAKE TOMORROW COME FASTER!

Love must be sincere. Hate what is evil; cling to what is good. Be devoted to one another in brotherly love. Honour one another above yourselves. Never be lacking in zeal, but keep your spiritual fervour, serving the Lord. Be joyful in hope, patient in affliction, faithful in prayer. Share with God's people who are in need. Practise hospitality.

ROMANS 12:9–13

The final chapters of Paul's letter to the Romans could be seen as volume 1 of *A Practical Handbook for Living the Christian Life*. Chapter 12 neatly unpacks what it means to live as a follower of Jesus in a world that does not, for the most part, share Christian values and vision. In these verses, and those surrounding them, Paul gives a checklist of 'Things to do while you wait'—in this case, waiting for Jesus' return. If we don't just sit there but do something, we might just make the waiting seem shorter, whatever we're waiting for.

When my children were younger, they often found Christmas Eve almost too long to bear. As I tucked them up in bed, they would plead with me to make the next day come faster. 'Promise it will be Christmas Day when we wake up, Mum. Promise!' they would cry. But of course I dared not, knowing full well that they were likely to fall asleep at 8pm but wake at five minutes to midnight. Over the years we developed a subtle routine to involve them in as many tiny tasks and preparations as possible, so that by the time they went to bed on Christmas Eve they would feel that they had done as much as possible to hasten that long-awaited special day, Christmas Day itself.

They began by helping with last-minute food preparations and a

125

special Christmas Eve tea. Then we'd take a walk to breathe in sleep-inducing (well, that was the theory) fresh air as it was getting dark. It was a chance to peer nosily into lighted windows at neighbours' Christmas trees, and to look up at the stars and wonder at the shepherds' awe and the wise men's leading. We would return to put a taper to the candle in the lantern we always leave outside in the tradition of a light to welcome the Christ-child and his family. Then it was bath-time, and afterwards the moment to open one special preview present of a book for bedtime—another family tradition. Finally, I would tell them that all they could do now was go off to bed as they were told, often with their new book tucked under their arms, and try to get some sleep. That would make the day come faster. This laborious final task, doubtless the most difficult of the day, was never faced with much enthusiasm, but at least they always felt that they had done all they could to speed things up. I could not 'speed' the arrival of Christmas Day, only structure and fill the children's waiting time, doubtless inadvertently increasing their excitement and anticipation along the way.

It's the same with all that God asks us to do as we wait for the fulfilment of his promises. Peter writes, 'You ought to live holy and godly lives as you look forward to the day of God and speed it's coming' (2 Peter 3:11b–12a). How patient are we as we trust in God's timing? How obedient in living godly lives? How anxious to do everything we can to hasten God's kingdom in all its marvellous glory? How might we resolve to make this Christmas a time of 'looking forward to the day of God'?

Reflect...

If you can, walk out under the stars tonight, or look out from a window at the sky. Contemplate the waiting shepherds... the wise men waiting to reach their destination... Mary and Joseph waiting for their child. Then picture, however you can, the whole world waiting in expectation.

God of surprises,
It was a night such as this:
dark, unsuspecting, ordinary,
the night you chose to send your Son,
tiny, helpless, yet saviour of the world.
You carefully chose those you would tell first,
knew who would receive the birth announcements,
who would welcome him and bring him gifts.
Thank you that you chose me too.
Now, whom must I tell?

DEBRA'S CHRISTMAS DAY ON THE OCEAN

After Jesus was born in Bethlehem in Judea, during the time of King Herod, Magi from the east came to Jerusalem and asked, 'Where is the one who has been born king of the Jews? We saw his star in the east and have come to worship him. When King Herod heard this he was disturbed, and all Jerusalem with him. When he had called together all the people's chief priests and teachers of the law, he asked them where the Christ was to be born. 'In Bethlehem in Judea,' they replied, 'for this is what the prophet has written:

> '"But you, Bethlehem, in the land of Judah,
>   are by no means least among the rulers of Judah;
>   for out of you will come a ruler
>   who will be the shepherd of my people Israel."'

Then Herod called the Magi secretly and found out from them the exact time the star had appeared.
MATTHEW 2:1–7

Last night you may have looked up into the starry sky and marvelled at its depth and its beauty, and wondered at the creator God who set the stars in space to give us such a stunning canopy. Imagine, then, what it is like to be at sea at night, in a rowing boat, with the stars above to guide you and remind you of the vastness of the heavens and the one who made them.

Debra Veal set out on 7 October 2001 with her husband Andrew in *Troika Transatlantic*, a specially designed rowing boat, to take part in a transatlantic rowing race, the Ward Evans Atlantic Rowing challenge. After just over a week at sea, Andrew felt unable to continue, having discovered an inexplicable and crippling fear of the open sea. Debra made the decision to carry on alone. Her voyage was characterized by long periods of waiting—not just waiting to be reunited with her family and friends at the end of her adventure but waiting for weather to change, parcels to be delivered by the race support crew, and calls to come through on her satellite phone. What follows is something of her experience of Christmas Day on the ocean.[7]

'The weeks leading up to Christmas were difficult. Loneliness set in, and I was often painfully aware of the contrast between my life at sea and the lives of family and friends at home. While Andrew spoke to dozens of business acquaintances at smart business lunches, I spoke to myself and, if he was in the mood, Woody, the ship's teddy bear.

'While Mum enjoyed her long-awaited treat of a QE2 cruise just before Christmas, with fine food and silverware at dinner, I was eating boil-in-the-bag rice with a plastic spoon. My brother pointed out that her excursion had cost a fraction of what it had cost me to get thus far.

'As I slid my way over the "thousand miles to go" mark a few days before Christmas, though, I felt a little more optimistic. A thousand miles may seem a long way still left to row, but with a total journey of just under 3000, the thought of having only hundreds of miles left to row, instead of thousands, was a fantastic one. I celebrated with a little packet of honey-roasted peanuts and a swig of purified sea water, lifting it in a "toast and roast" gesture. Who needs Moet and caviar?

'Christmas Day was wonderful, largely due to the forethought of my twin sister, Hayley, who had orchestrated the biggest double binliner-full of goodies ever seen mid-Atlantic. It had been delivered a week or so before, by a couple of guys from the support yacht that followed the race, and was so overflowing with presents, cards and food that I had to repack *Troika* to fit it all in.

'So Christmas morning saw me with the para-anchor out, sitting out headwinds that were forecast until Boxing Day. It took me two hours, surrounded by "Troika blue" tinsel to match the boat, just to open all the cards and read the messages they contained. Presents included a beautiful turtle-shaped necklace from Andrew, a Christmas pudding, and the words of "My favourite things" from *The Sound of Music*, from my brother Matt. He thoughtfully considered that I might be missing the chance to watch it on TV! Phone calls to and from family—including Andrew, of course—followed. I didn't feel as homesick as I'd anticipated, and Andrew, now back in England, sounded happy. He was enjoying his niece's and nephew's Christmas toys and looking forward to a traditional lunch. I told him I was looking forward to chicken cuppa-soup!

'Mum was with my brothers in Devon, and Hayley and her husband were enjoying the sight of reindeer in snowy weather beside a loch in Scotland—weather that contrasted heavily with the climate in my part of the wide, wet world. Christmas Day had started stormy with headwinds, but by mid-afternoon the winds had dramatically changed direction, so I rowed through the afternoon in bright sunshine, wearing a bikini and Santa hat and singing "Raindrops on roses and whiskers on kittens", for which I now had all the words, thanks to Matt. I later discovered that Andrew had made me the focus of his prayer at the Christmas morning church service, and that he had prayed for tailwinds to return so that I could get a move on. His prayer was answered: they did return, just long enough for me to have an enjoyable and productive Christmas Day row.

'I ate my Christmas pudding while watching the sun set and realized there would never be another Christmas Day quite like it. The night sky that followed the sunset was, as ever, breathtaking. The stars are so bright above the Atlantic. There is, of course, no light pollution to dim their glow or fight for attention—no neon signs or fog lamps; just pure, clear light. The Milky Way and other star systems can be seen in all their glory. Sometimes the sky looked so full of stars, I expected it to burst at any minute. It was the shooting stars, though, that always held my attention, streaking across the blackness in their thousands. The larger ones left glowing trails across the skies, just like the start of a Disney movie.

'The night sky reminded me that I was just a tiny speck, not just in a vast ocean but in a vast creation. It brought with it that feeling of utter contentment and grace that became my companion so often. Yes, I thought of Andrew, of Hayley, Mum and my brothers and the friends who were rooting for me, and I cast my mind forward to the finish I dreamt of so often. I imagined how it would be to see them all again—not to have to wait for the wind to change, for snatches of conversation on the satellite phone or for dawn to end the lonely darkness and allow me to row on. But I had to admit that if you were going to spend Christmas Day alone, rowing in the middle of the Atlantic beneath the starry heavens was a pretty good way to do it!'

Debra's journey came to an end, her dream fulfilled, her waiting over, when she rowed into Port St Charles, Barbados, on 26 January 2002, after 112 days at sea. Andrew, her friends and family were waiting for her on the quayside with a banner: 'Come in Number 22, your time is up!'

Reflect…

'The future belongs to those who lay hold of their God-given dreams'
(Anon).

Father God,
set a dream in my heart.
Help me trace its detail
from small beginnings;
colour it with bold brush strokes.
Engrave it on my heart
in times of doubt.

Strengthen its design against
the winds of impossibility.
Give me arms outstretched to catch the dreams of others.
Help us sketch hope in
the aftermath of pain;
stand together in the
shadows of disappointment;
share in celebration
as dreams become reality.

Creator God, set a dream
in my heart…
a dream of hope,
a dream that will change
a moment,
a day,
a life,
for eternity.[8]

A PROMISE KEPT–A LONG WAIT OVER

Now there was a man in Jerusalem called Simeon, who was righteous and devout. He was waiting for the consolation of Israel, and the Holy Spirit was upon him. It had been revealed to him by the Holy Spirit that he would not die before he had seen the Lord's Christ. Moved by the Spirit, he went into the temple courts. When the parents brought in the child Jesus to do for him what the custom of the Law required, Simeon took him in his arms and praised God, saying:

'Sovereign Lord, as you have promised,
you now dismiss your servant in peace.
For my eyes have seen your salvation,
which you have prepared in the sight of all people,
a light for revelation to the Gentiles
and for glory to your people Israel.'

LUKE 2:25–32

God's people have always been encouraged to wait patiently in the midst of their current circumstances. Forty-three times in the Old Testament alone they are asked to 'wait on the Lord'. The Old Testament promised that a Messiah would come, and the world waited centuries for that promise to be fulfilled. Yet when he finally came, as that helpless babe you might have sung about in traditional carols at church yesterday, he was barely recognized—and only then by those who had never given up hope during the long years of waiting, like Simeon.

I am always very moved by the story of Simeon. I imagine him

133

praying daily for the Messiah, calling on his God persistently for the one his people needed so badly. I often wonder if, in his earnestness and desire, he wept and asked God for reassurance; and if God, with the tenderness of a Father, said through his Holy Spirit, 'Don't worry, Simeon, I promise you will see him before you die.' And now, here, on an ordinary day much like any other, the Holy Spirit prompts Simeon to go into the temple courts and there before his eyes is the Messiah he has prayed and waited for. He praises God, knowing that he can now die in peace, and leaves Mary with a prophetic word: 'And a sword will pierce your own soul too' (Luke 2:35), a first indication of Jesus' future suffering.

What gave Simeon hope through those long years of waiting? Did he imagine the day when the Messiah would be revealed to him? Had God given him any glimpse of what might lie ahead? One thing is certain: Simeon, like Abraham before him, believed all he had been promised. He waited patiently, and his faithfulness was rewarded by the child he 'took into his arms' (v. 28).

I wonder if you watched a child unwrap a Christmas parcel yesterday. Children are not great at waiting. If there's a present to be opened, it really is best to open it now. The suspense is too much to bear. Once a shiny wrapped gift is in their clutches, they will waste not a moment, pulling at ribbon, tearing at paper, struggling with tape, until finally all is revealed and the contents are well and truly unwrapped. And then—they look round for the next! As they get older, the unwrapping slows down a little. They may develop tactics, opening the one they think is likely to be most uninteresting first—the socks from Auntie or the dictionary from Dorothy next door—and leaving the very best till last. Or they squeeze a parcel to guess at its contents, even peeping into the half-unwrapped folds to glimpse what is waiting to be revealed.

Now that my children are in their teenage years, they take some delight in *not* opening their gifts too early. Our local church follows the tradition, during its Christmas morning family service, of gathering the children to the front to show their favourite presents to the assembled church family, while bleary-eyed parents, still suffering from their early morning start, look on. When he was young, our son felt somewhat cheated not to have opened more than the tiny gifts and sweets in his stocking by this stage. Cruel parents that we are, we decided that the real reason for the season should come first—that of celebrating the birth of Jesus. We always wait until after church to unwrap our main presents. Our son soon realized, however, that the other children at church had already received the best, whereas he still had it all to come! Last year he suggested we leave the gifts until Boxing Day—quite happy to delay the opening as long as possible and just enjoy the anticipation.

It is a sign of maturity to be able to wait for unseen things, and a greater one to understand that we often gain more from the wait than from the 'getting there', especially if God is teaching us on the way. We grow by learning to trust his perspective, his choices and his timing. Effectively he is asking us to wait for him. Like Simeon's, our wait may be long—but we will not be disappointed. Let's learn to enjoy the anticipation.

Reflect...

What have you waited for endlessly... and yet still wait for? Bring the complex emotions attached to that wait before God and ask him to reassure you and give you patience.

Father God, my heart has known your salvation. Reveal more of it to me as I wait in anticipation, patience and trust.

ON EAGLE'S WINGS:
FROM PATIENCE TO HOPE

Do you not know?
Have you not heard?
The Lord is the everlasting God,
the Creator of the ends of the earth.
He will not grow tired or weary,
and his understanding no one can fathom.
He gives strength to the weary
and increases the power of the weak.
Even youths grow tired and weary,
and young men stumble and fall;
but those who hope in the Lord
will renew their strength.
They will soar on wings like eagles;
they will run and not grow weary,
they will walk and not be faint.

ISAIAH 40:28–31

Because 'his understanding no one can fathom' (v. 28), we may often find that our patience in waiting matures into a greater hope. We do not understand God's ways, but we know God, and therefore we have hope. In the Authorized Version of the Bible, the word 'wait' is used in verse 31 instead of 'hope': 'those who wait on the Lord...' There is room for both. Waiting and hope sit together, because hope itself is waiting and believing that the better, if not the best, is yet to be.

The Christmas season often gives us an opportunity to watch those films we've seen 20 times before but don't mind seeing yet again! For me, David Puttnam's film *Chariots of Fire*, set in the 1920s, is a favourite. In the film, Olympic athlete Eric Liddell reads this passage from Isaiah aloud, from the Authorized Version. Liddell, a committed Christian played by actor Ian Charleson, is taking part in a Church of Scotland Sunday morning service in Paris. He has refused to run in a qualifying race for the Olympics on a Sunday—'the Lord's Day'—facing much ridicule and misunderstanding in the process. If you know the film, you will remember that, as he reads the words in his warm Scottish accent, the film cuts to his fellow athletes, who are running their own qualifying races a short distance away. The contrast is striking. Eric Liddell reads out the words from Isaiah, strong and sure in his faith. He is upright, confident. At the same time, his fellow Olympic athletes are seen crashing painfully to the ground in slow motion. They send grazing gravel flying into a grey sky, console one another in despair and defeat and are seen dripping and desolate after heavy rain hits the track. Liddell goes on to run his qualifying race on another day, thanks to the generosity of another athlete, winning his race and his medal.

Look closely at these verses, however, and you notice that those who hope in the Lord will not always soar like an eagle. They can, and they will, but they will not always be asked to do so. Sometimes running will be what God requires. At other times they may only be able to walk, yet, however weak, they will not grow faint. Walking will be enough.

Those words remind me of one long night in hospital for cancer treatment. I was confined to an isolation room with a tiny bathroom after a stem cell transplant. During the night I had made the difficult short journey, weak from sickness and illness, into the bathroom. Sitting there to try to regain strength to walk back to the bed, two IV drip stands in tow, I realized that I would not make it—especially knowing that within a few minutes I would need to make the journey yet again. Then I remembered that there is power and strength in the name of Jesus and in hoping in the Lord. So, in the quiet and semi-darkness, I began to whisper his name again and again as I waited. It was all I felt able to do.

I can barely describe what happened as I waited and whispered. I felt that although I was still sitting exactly where I was, I was somehow being lifted out of the weakness itself and given a few minutes relief from the awfulness of it all. After a short while, with the presence of Jesus still very real, I realized that I had regained at least some of my strength, and was able to creep slowly back to the bed, dragging my companion IV drip stands behind me. I had walked—just—and had not grown faint. The running and soaring would have to wait! I went to sleep and slept deeply and well for the first time in a long night. I had hoped in and waited on the Lord, and he had literally renewed my strength.

Wherever we are as we wait on him, it is best done in his time and strength. Spiritually soaring when he points to the heavens, running without growing weary because he has set the pace and walking when we are weak, in the knowledge that he will not let us faint.

Reflect...

Look back on times when God has asked you to walk, run, even soar in your Christian life, and then at those times when you have only been able to crawl. How did your relationship with him differ on each occasion?

Lord, I come to you, let my heart be changed, renewed,
Flowing from the grace that I found in you.
Lord, I've come to know the weaknesses you see in me
Will be stripped away, by the power of your love.

Hold me close, let your love surround me,
Bring me near, draw me to your side.
And as I wait I'll rise up like the eagle,
And I will soar with you, your Spirit leads me on
In the power of your love.

Lord, unveil my eyes, let me see you face to face,
The knowledge of your love as you live in me.
Lord, renew my mind as your will unfolds in my life,
Living every day in the power of your love.

GEOFF BULLOCK

WAITING ON GOD

But you, dear friends, build yourselves up in your most holy faith and pray in the Holy Spirit. Keep yourselves in God's love as you wait for the mercy of our Lord Jesus Christ to bring you to eternal life. Be merciful to those who doubt; snatch others from the fire and save them; to others show mercy, mixed with fear—hating even the clothing stained by corrupted flesh.

To him who is able to keep you from falling and to present you before his glorious presence without fault and with great joy—to the only God our saviour be glory, majesty, power and authority, through Jesus Christ our Lord, before all ages, now and forevermore! Amen.

JUDE 20–25

These words are a simple and beautiful picture of a Christian community living with each other, living in the presence of God and reaching out to those around them who are lost. Bear these verses from Jude in mind throughout this meditation.

Imagine yourself in each of the following environments.

You are waiting in the quiet of your favourite room at home.

The quiet might be rare—a privilege; or common—a burden.

In your imagination, look around at your belongings. Identify one or two. What do they mean to you?

How might they help you 'wait on God'?

What might God be saying about this place?

Whom would he have you welcome here?

You are waiting at the edge of your church fellowship.

In your imagination look around. Notice your closest friends, and those you do not yet know.

Watch the chat and laughter of small groups, the play of children.

Is anyone alone?

Does anyone call across to you?

What might God be saying to you as you wait?

Where will you go next? To whom will you go?

You are waiting at the open doorway of your home.

In your imagination, look out into the street, across balconies or pathways.

Watch the comings and goings, the busyness or stillness.

What do you want to do next? Will you close the door and stay inside, or step beyond it?

Where would you walk to now if you had the choice? Follow that walk in your imagination.

Where will you finish your walk? Or where will you stay?

What might God be saying to you in this place?

You are waiting in a wide, open space. Picture it—perhaps a beach you know, a field, or a park.

In your imagination, look around you. Notice what you may have missed before.

Look a long way off, as far as your eye can see.

Look up at the sky. Are there clouds, or is the sky clear?

Do you shield your eyes against the sun, or your face against the wind?

Feel the ground beneath your feet. Is it grass, sand, or gravel?

Look ahead now and imagine Jesus walking towards you, his arms outstretched. He knows you have been waiting for him.

What will you say?

What will he say?

Reflect...

As you reflect on this week's readings, ask yourself a few questions about your 'wait on the Lord'. Record your responses in your notebook and perhaps write a prayer to set those responses before God. Ask yourself:

- *Am I really waiting for him or is he waiting for me?*
- *What is he saying about my 'waiting place'?*
- *Am I learning from the wait? Is the anticipation a joy?*
- *Am I obedient as I wait in my spiritual life: In my relationship with him? By persevering in faith? In loving others? By letting him set the pace?*
- *Do I take time to gaze in wonder at his glory?*
- *Have I set my dreams before him?*
- *Do I really believe that he will do all he promises as the old year ends and a new one begins?*

Lord, help me wait—
in patience,
in anticipation,
in obedience,
in wonder at your glory—
with my dreams laid out before you,
at peace in your timing
and
believing in your promises.

✣

HOPING IN THINGS UNSEEN

GALLERY: 'AFTER THE STORM'

A woman is standing on cobbles, leaning against a rough harbour wall, looking out to sea. Lobster pots, nets and heavy rope lie at her feet. It is early morning. This is the calm after the storm. One or two fishing boats, recently returned, hug the quayside as if in relief and gratitude. Fishermen are unloading their catch, sharing tales of the night's fishing, gesticulating past fears.

This is a Victorian painting, in the style of the Newlyn School, a group of painters based in the Cornish fishing town of the same name. It is typical of the domestic scenes popular at the time. The setting is slightly romanticized, attempting to portray reality but heavy with emotion. It is painted mainly in blues and greys. Great sweeps of grey oils and filigree patterns of pure white give the sea its mood. The gentle blotted light of the early hours and delicately drawn detail lend it intimacy.

The woman is tall, strong, but obviously weary. Her hair is pinned up but unruly strands have escaped and lie around her shoulders. She wears a grey-blue dress of a coarse, heavy fabric and a white apron. She hugs a thick shawl around her shoulders to keep out the chill: she looks as if she has been standing in this one place for some time.

On one side of the painting, set further back, a group of older women are talking together, heads bowed, looking in her direction. One of them is weeping; another points towards the sea.

Returning your gaze to the watching woman, you notice that beneath her shawl she clasps a small bundle. It is a sleeping infant, wrapped warm, secure and tight against her breast. It is as if the woman is holding on to the newness of this little life with every waiting breath.

You lift your eyes and look more closely at her face. A dark shadow is behind her, but her face is lit, turned to the far horizon where the risen sun has lit the water in a pool of yellow light beneath a bank of cloud. There are no familiar shapes illuminated there indicating a returning fishing boat. The flat pool of light is empty.

Her face, half-turned seawards, is resolved, determined. She *will* wait, however long it takes. She will not turn back into the dark shadow that is the threshold of the house, or close its door on her hope. Her skin is pale but slightly flushed by the breeze and salt air; her chin is slightly lifted as if in defiance. Her lips are held tightly together, but it is her eyes that speak. They are the same blue and grey as the sea, stirred up in the same way, with the ebb and flow of emotion. The long wait has left within them the 'last watch' of patience and the brightness of hope clouded only by fear. A speck is all she longs to see—a tiny familiar speck of a boat in the pool of yellow light laid out along the horizon like a cloth. The artist could have painted such a speck, could have brightened hope with a brush stroke—but he has chosen not to do so.

You know that the woman is hoping that if she waits and watches, the speck will become a boat, and the boat will be recognized, and her eyes will close with a sigh in relief and thanksgiving.

As you walk away, you know she will go on waiting, however long it takes.

INTRODUCTION

So much of our Christmas celebration depends on careful planning and good preparation. There are the ten dozen mince pies to bake, the nativity play to rehearse, cards to write and, if you're like me, countless lists to make, most of which get forgotten anyway. Then there's that culinary work of art, 'The Christmas Dinner', which most of us are fortunate enough to share.

I enjoy all the preparation—the endless vegetable peeling I've already mentioned, the table decoration—although I always emerge from the kitchen at the end of it all looking as if I've spent the last few hours in a sauna. The truth is, in order to present that fabulous Christmas lunch, I have to work hard and long.

In the execution of every art form there is some groundwork, something laborious or painstaking, something at which we have to persevere, and perspire. Often this is the part without which the whole work would be meaningless, lifeless or would simply fall flat.

Faith is the groundwork for hope and, hand in hand with patience, builds our waiting skills as we hope for the 'things unseen' (2 Corinthians 4:18). We may feel we have no reason to hope, but the human spirit often has the capacity to go on hoping when all hope should, logically, be gone. Paradoxically, 'hope' is a word we use lightly. Its use has been trivialized, reducing its emotive strength in the process: 'I hope it doesn't rain'; 'I hope there's not more turkey for tea'; 'I hope he likes the sweater'. While Christmas shopping in a department store recently, I even noticed a skin cream called 'Hope in a Jar'.

'Hope' has become a word used with a hint of false anxiety, a crossing of fingers, a wobble of confidence or a lukewarm optimism. Yet hope is perhaps the most life-giving and powerful force in human nature, undoubtedly God-given. It draws us towards our true home and to the one we hope for—sometimes without our even realizing we hold such hope.

This week, as we contemplate the new year ahead, we'll be reflecting on the nature of hope—personal hope; the way God keeps hope alive in us when we have all but buried it; and what happens when life is so tough that we are hoping almost against hope.

Hope makes us ask so many questions. How do we cling to hope in the midst of suffering? How might hope transform our lives when we feel we have little more than hope to cling to? When we are in pain, or have our faces turned to the wall in despair, the tiny flicker of light that is hope must get our attention. It must be fanned into life, lest our spirit die with the flame.

How does hope keep our eyes watching an open door as we long for the homecoming of a loved one, or for reconciliation with one from whom we are estranged? So many of us know what it is like to ache for a 'prodigal'—a son, daughter or other family member whom we would love to see walk through the door and into our arms. Does hope hasten their coming? Or is it in vain? How is our hope in life itself woven together with a longing for faithfulness, of a kind only God can promise?

Our eternal hope is in him, and his hope is in us. His longing for reconciliation with us, his children, can transform our lives. Ultimately, hope is all we have—yet hope in God is all we need.

WHAT IS HOPE?

But the eyes of the Lord are on those who fear him,
on those whose hope is in his unfailing love,
to deliver them from death and keep them alive in famine.
We wait in hope for the Lord;
he is our help and our shield.
In him our hearts rejoice,
for we trust in his holy name.
May your unfailing love rest upon us, O Lord,
even as we put our hope in you.

PSALM 33:18–22

Waiting and hope are woven together in the words of this psalm. It is as if one cannot exist without the other. The psalmist begins by praising God for the works of his hands, his creativity, his power and his faithfulness to his chosen people. In doing so, he lays the foundation of memories for the building of hope. 'Look,' he says, 'see what he has made; remember what he has done; recall how he has been faithful—and for this reason he can be trusted.' These final verses of the psalm almost creak with the sturdiness and strength of their faith-filled words. Twice they speak of God's love as 'unfailing', and it is in this unfailing love that our hope is to be found and can equally be invested. It is in that hope that we are able to wait, in trust and confidence.

Hope is often the last resource we have left. Heroic stories of rescue and survival frequently ring with the words, 'We did not give up hope', as if hope was life itself, and the very act of hanging on to it, against the odds, would ensure survival.

Roberto Benigni's award-winning film, *Life Is Beautiful*, is partly set in the last months of World War II. Guido, an Italian Jew, Dora his wife and their son Giosue are sent to a concentration camp. In an effort to protect his son from the horrors that await him, Guido turns the experience of the journey and life in the camp into an elaborate game of challenge, skill, nerve and endurance. He explains to the bewildered but intrigued Giosue that points can be scored for successful completion of each part of the 'game' and that the ultimate reward is a ride on a life-size tank—the prize for which Giosue longs.

Concealing his son in various locations, and spinning him a tale of their soon-to-be-enjoyed triumph as winners of the game, Guido eventually saves Giosue's life by hiding him in a tiny cupboard to await the liberation of the camp by the Americans. Although Guido is tragically shot in those final days, his hope is fulfilled at the end of the film, as Giosue is carried to his mother's arms, and freedom, via a ride on the tank of his American liberator.

It is a wonderful film—even if it is an unbelievable fable—of a father instilling hope at all costs. Yet Giosue's hope is built, albeit unknown to him, on fantasy. Christian hope can often seem the same—and not just to those outside the faith. But Christian hope is much more. It does not involve living in a blind fantasy, for us or for others. It is not a grim-faced determination to hang on to the last piece of flotsam in the shipwreck of life. Neither is it a jolly enthusiasm banging away like a drum, deafening us to the pain and suffering of our peers, or a false or fragile confidence that is fleeting, always changing with the wind or our many moods. It is a solid assurance of the presence of God, both in this life and the next—not 'pie in the sky when you die', or even 'cake on a plate as we wait'—but something far more substantial, trustworthy, life-giving and eternal.

It is the hope God places in our hearts for him—the hope of his presence, his eternal life, his goodness and protection, certainly, but also 'something more'. It's 'something more' that is almost tangible, yet just out of reach. It is like something delicious we taste, but with a wonderful flavour that we cannot place. Like the top note in an exquisite piece of music that has us yearning in a way that we cannot explain, we only know that it moves us to tears. The hope of God is like a chase in the dark, where we almost catch the hem of his garment but not quite. He will keep us guessing and longing and chasing after him in the midst of it—but not in vain. One day he will let us catch him and will turn and hold us closer than we have ever been held. Then our hope will be fulfilled.

Reflect...

The word which God has written on the brow of every man is 'hope'.
VICTOR HUGO

Lord, as I wait, give me rejoicing in my heart, hope as its companion, and rest your unfailing love upon me. I wait… and put all my hope in the reality of you.

HOPE IN DARKNESS

Therefore, since we have been justified through faith, we have peace with God through our Lord Jesus Christ, through whom we have gained access by faith into this grace in which we now stand. And we rejoice in the hope of the glory of God. Not only so, but we also rejoice in our sufferings, because we know that suffering produces perseverance; perseverance, character; and character, hope. And hope does not disappoint us, because God has poured out his love into our hearts by the Holy Spirit, whom he has given us.

ROMANS 5:1–5

What if we are suffering as we wait, or wrestling with disappointment? How can we embrace hope from a dark waiting place? There is no more painful wait than one that is marked by suffering: the wait of one in agonies of sickness, the wait of a parent for a prodigal child, the wait of one anxious for news of a missing, 'presumed dead', relative or friend. It is as if no one can ever really understand. Isolation adds to our pain; torment scores deep scars into our suffering; tears are like torrents.

I struggle when I see Paul's words 'we also rejoice in our sufferings' used out of context. So often they are bandied about to justify a stiff-upper-lip, sackcloth-and-ashes kind of spirituality—a steely-eyed endurance that I am sure God does not intend us to adopt, let alone rejoice in. They are even used to promote a 'life is awful, but hallelujah!' insensitivity, which makes those who are hurting hurt more. It is only when the words are put into context that we can understand what Paul is getting at.

If any group of people ever knew a lot about waiting in hope, it was the early Church. They knew what it was to look beyond the real practical difficulties they were facing, to an eternal hope. But they also knew something of the way suffering and perseverance can develop Christian character—not making them into stoical 'chuck it all at me, I can take it' saints who just love being kicked when they're down, but those who can see the potential for looking upward into the face of God and knowing him more deeply and intimately in the midst of suffering.

Most Christians will admit that it is in the difficult times that their faith has grown, not the times of prosperity or success. Some may even get to the point where they almost welcome the suffering —not for its own sake but for what it produces, because their memory of the positive faith impact it had last time round is a strangely precious one.

Recently, in the midst of a 'Christianity Explored' course discussion, I was asked by a member of the group whether my experience of cancer had made me doubt. I didn't want to hijack the discussion for long, so simply shook my head enthusiastically. Intrigued at this, the group pressed me to explain. I told them that while I would not wish to face the horrors of those years again, with their awful and debilitating treatment, from a faith perspective it was the best thing that has ever happened to me. Staggered, they asked why. I explained that I had been very seriously ill, and that in the midst of that awfulness it was God whom I clung to. The medical odds meant that I knew my life was in his hands and there was nowhere else to go. God was much more able to communicate with me—and did so—because my sole focus was his love for me and his purpose in what I was going through.

Bishop James Jones, reflecting on Psalm 22 ('My God, My God, why have you forsaken me?') writes, 'It is in the moment of desolation that the sufferer binds himself fastly to God... in spite of the catastrophes surrounding him, God was still "My God..."'[9] We can know a greater depth of relationship and understanding of our need of him, as well as his greatness, from what we learn in dark times. Far from separating us from God, suffering can draw us closer through an experience that will help us identify with his choice to enter the world and suffer because he loved us.

Of course, it doesn't help to be told all that in the midst of suffering. As Joni Eareckson Tada says, 'When your heart is wrung out like a sponge, an orderly list of "16 good Biblical reasons why this is happening" can sting like salt in a wound. You don't stop bleeding that way.'[10] Neat answers are rarely enough. It can sometimes be enough to remember that while others may disappoint us, with their glib answers, their lack of faithfulness and their well-meant platitudes, God won't. He may seem silent for a time. He may quietly hold our hand in the waiting darkness. But eventually he will emerge from the gloom and help us look beyond suffering and disappointment and into the light.

In his marvellous book *Beyond the Clouds*, Laurence Singlehurst writes on pain and disillusionment:

God does not wave a magic wand that removes all these things as if they were never there. The important thing is to move them to one side so that you can see the sun—to live in the power of your dreams and expectations, rather than being shaped by the cloud.[11]

He admits, however, that 'even just moving them is not an easy task'. God is working out his plan in each of our lives. He is in control and his promises can be relied upon. Part of faith is acknowledging that it will not always be easy to believe that. If we can believe, however, that the issue is not whether we can carry on feeling overflowing with faith as we wait but whether God remains in control, we can still have hope. Writer Jenny Francis comments:

Perhaps there are times on life's journey when we feel alienated from God and can only cling on to what we know intellectually, and it is as much as we can do to exercise the discipline of faith. This can be so painful. Yet somewhere in the deep recesses of the mind and heart we know we are not forgotten... There is always, even in the darkest reaches of my night, a slender golden thread somewhere which makes it bearable.[12]

Perhaps that slender golden thread might be made of hope—the hope that will never disappoint us. I believe that God particularly treasures such a golden thread and that he holds the other end tightly, day and night, from this year-end into the next, through all eternity.

Reflect...

When did you—at last—see a tiny glimmer of hope in the darkness? Did you recognize God as its source?

Lord, sometimes I feel as if I am hanging on to hope with that tiny thread. Surely, I think, it will break at any moment, snap under pressure, be blown aside and out of reach by the lightest breeze, and my grip will falter through the long days of waiting.

Help me remember that the other end is held tightly by you in one hand, and that if I fall you will catch me in the palm of the other, even as you sit silently alongside me in the darkness.

CRANING OUR NECKS
AND STANDING ON TIPTOE

Out of the depths I cry to you, O Lord;
O Lord, hear my voice.
Let your ears be attentive
to my cry for mercy.
If you, O Lord, kept a record of sins,
O Lord, who could stand?
But with you there is forgiveness;
therefore you are feared.
I wait for the Lord, my soul waits,
and in his word I put my hope.
My soul waits for the Lord
more than watchmen wait for the morning,
more than watchmen wait for the morning.
O Israel, put your hope in the Lord,
for with the Lord is unfailing love
and with him is full redemption.
He himself will redeem Israel
from all their sins.

PSALM 130

In Old Testament times, watchmen played a vital role, not just in the defence of walled cities but by warning of approaching messengers or in defending important sites, especially those of economic value. Stationed high on a city wall or the uppermost part of a building, a watchman's wait was undoubtedly a cold and lonely one. He dare not allow himself to snooze, as he had to remain continually alert for fear of missing any sound or movement that might indicate an approach. Only the welcome light of the dawn brought his wait to an end.

Here, David, in his anxiety for God's forgiveness and mercy, imagines himself in a similar state of waiting. He is craning his neck as he looks out along the battlements of his life for the light of the Lord's presence and the longed-for redemption that will end his watch. We can almost hear David's yearning in his repetition of verse 6: 'more than watchmen wait for the morning, more than watchmen wait for the morning'.

His is a wait from night till daybreak. When we are waiting anxiously for God to work in our lives, for circumstances to change or for our needs to be met in some way, our wait too can be a cold and lonely one. We may cry to God 'out of the depths' and then feel that there is little more we can do but wait in our exposed and lonely place, exhausted and longing for the peace of sleep, until he appears like the welcome dawn.

One of the most difficult things about diagnosis and treatment for cancer is the waiting. It's how I came to choose the subject of this book, and how I have learnt so much about the parallels of waiting that exist in our spiritual lives (although, I fear I still have much to learn).

Many of you reading these words will know the way the waiting goes, and David Noble shared something of it in his story on pages 67 to 69. Initially there's a wait for the results of a barrage of tests, then for the real diagnosis and the 'I'm afraid it is' conversation. Then follows waiting for treatment, waiting while you're having treatment, even waiting for the bus or train home afterwards. Even when the treatment is finally over, when everything possible has been done, there's the waiting to see if it's all been worthwhile, waiting to discover whether remission can be declared and anything like normal life can be reclaimed. There's a strange tension between wanting life to return to normal and knowing that this could be a risky business, because just as you begin to live life normally the cancer could pop up like an unwelcome April Fool and be back.

Gradually, though, like a sleepy welcome dawn, we become aware that there is a ray of hope stronger than has been seen for some time—a hope that dares to show us that we can look further ahead along the road than we have previously dared. At the time of writing, my consultant has decided that I needn't visit the hospital for six months, unless I notice any symptoms that bother me. It is a huge and liberating leap from the three-monthly gaps between appointments that I'd known before. As I stand on the battlements of *my* life, I can straighten up a bit and dare to look more confidently ahead. An ambush by the disease that has attacked my life is a little less likely. There may be a bit of a 'no man's land' of remission to wander across, but I thank God for his unfailing love. Every New Year is a gift.

Today is New Year's Eve and, like me, you may be planning to attend a watchnight service. It's a time to 'pray out' the old year and look forward to what lies ahead in the dawning of a new year. Sometimes we may have to apply the principles of a watchnight service to the dark times in our lives—to throw off the shadows of all we've left behind and put our hope in God's word, like watchmen who wait for the morning and trust in his unfailing love.

Reflect...

Take up your notebook, and think back over the past year. Offer to God both those memories that bring joy... and those that bring pain... in thanksgiving and surrender. Resolve to 'throw off the shadows' and welcome the dawn.

David says that he puts his hope in God's word. How might we do that?

- *Through the study of his word, the Bible*
- *Through meditating on its truths*
- *Through listening to God, to ourselves, to others*
- *By remembering his promises*

Resolve, this New Year, to make the study of and reflection on God's word part of your essential 'skill building' as you learn the art of waiting.

Almighty and everlasting God, your word spoke the very beginning of time. Your name grants its sunrise and sunset, endorses its passing and details its future. As I wait for the morning, remind me that you are also in the darkness with me, and that I can hope in your word as in the certainty of dawn.

A PROMISE OF FAITHFULNESS

The Lord is gracious and compassionate,
slow to anger and rich in love.
The Lord is good to all;
he has compassion on all he has made.
All you have made will praise you, O Lord;
your saints will extol you.
They will tell of the glory of your kingdom
and speak of your might,
so that all men may know of your mighty acts
and the glorious splendour of your kingdom.
Your kingdom is an everlasting kingdom,
and your dominion endures through all generations.
The Lord is faithful to all his promises
and loving toward all he has made.

PSALM 145:8–13

David paints us a fabulous picture of the might, greatness, goodness
and security of God. He reminds us that God's rule is indisputable
and that his kingdom is everlasting. That's a good few things to
remember on New Year's Day! These confident words lie in strong,
clear contrast to the gentleness and assurance of the words in the last
two lines, 'The Lord is faithful to all his promises and loving toward
all he has made', but in truth they qualify and underpin them.

Faithfulness is becoming a rare commodity. Marriage seems to
have become an 'easy in, easier out' option based increasingly on
contract and pre-nuptial agreement more than on love, commit-
ment and faithfulness. In 1999 there were 145,000 divorces in the

UK and it is predicted that, on current trends, just over two out of five marriages will ultimately end in divorce. Similar figures assume that 28 per cent of children will experience the divorce of their parents before their 16th birthday.[13]

A promise of faithfulness is all too easily broken, and the hope it contained is dashed in the storm of marriage breakdown. Paradoxically, marriage is on the increase and gaining in popularity, as more and more of us hope for security and faithfulness for ever with the one we love. Others will know only too well the pain and bewilderment of unfaithfulness, the sense of rejection and the ache of loneliness that accompany the fall-out. Some find it impossible to trust again, preferring to remain alone in the hope of protecting themselves in their vulnerability. Others never give up the hope of faithfulness, marrying again and again, and always genuinely believing that 'this time' will be different. The actress and singer Jennifer Lopez was quoted as saying, after her second marriage and while contemplating a third, that she had never been in a 'proper marriage' before. It seemed as if each time she was hoping for something more, a faithfulness and constancy that she had been unable to maintain.

Recently, when travelling home by train, I noticed a discarded 'celebrity' magazine. The front-page headlines and straplines were exclusively about faithfulness, and featured the marriage and relationship breakdowns of a number of high-profile media couples. One celebrity husband was quoted as saying, 'I forgive Zoe her affair'; another wife on the verge of marriage breakdown appealed, 'I want Jude to love me'; while the headline ran, 'Brad and Jennifer in marriage split shock'. Even in our cynical media-driven world, faithfulness is so important—even if that importance is unspoken—that unfaithfulness is news.

We could certainly believe that there must be an intrinsic reason why, as humans, we place our hope in a 'special someone' whom we love so easily and place all our hope upon. Yet often we have that hope painfully dashed when relationships crumble, and life and love aren't all we hoped they would be. What is it that calls us to a hope of faithfulness? Perhaps we each contain a hidden spiritual compass that points us heavenward to the one whose faithfulness will be secure and whose promises will never be broken. Perhaps it's our heavenly homing device, designed to protect us from placing too much hope in that much-loved but all-too-human 'special some-one' who cannot deliver, and to turn our eyes upon the one who really does know and love us best.

Our material lives promise much and deliver little, like the packaging on the specially marketed Christmas gift packs that many of us will have thrown out with the wrapping paper last week. So much effort is put into a Christmas theme and an appealing container, purely with the purpose of selling the contents over a relatively short marketing period. We may place too much hope in the ability of such marketing to fulfil our dream of what magazines, with their tips for food, drink and decorations, promise will be our 'best Christmas ever'. The appeal doesn't last long because, of course, we are looking in the wrong place for the promise to be fulfilled.

For those of us blessed with more than enough to eat, feasting and fun should be seen as added blessings, not the focal point, yet it is easy to be fooled by the promise of a 'complete Christmas experience'. In the 1970s sitcom, *The Good Life*, the affluent Margot orders her 'entire Christmas' from a large store—tree, food, drink and decorations. But when the order is delivered on Christmas Eve, she discovers that the tree is a few inches too short, and sends her entire delivery back in protest, completely forgetting that there can be no replacement as the next day is Christmas Day. At first she announces to husband Jerry that Christmas is cancelled, but later accepts an invitation from next-door neighbours Tom and Barbara, whose much simpler approach to Christmas saves the day and teaches Margot a little more about true promise.

One of my lifelong favourite poems is by Robert Frost. 'Stopping by Woods on a Snowy Evening'[14] is short, simple and somewhat sentimental, but I can recite it in my sleep! The poet is travelling some distance by horse and trap and stops near a wood belonging to an acquaintance, in the midst of a snowfall, to 'watch his woods fill up with snow'. The picture Robert Frost paints entranced me as a child, and still does now—his dreamy picture of 'easy wind and downy flake'. But the lines that always kept me guessing, imagining welcoming cottage windows and loving arrivals home, were the final ones: 'but I have promises to keep, and miles to go before I sleep…' The idea that the traveller was committed to travelling so far in a snowfall with the declared intent of keeping promises, the contents of which I could only wonder at, always warmed my heart and filled me with excitement.

Our heavenly Father has promises to keep, and we can be assured that he will keep them with faithfulness. His promises and faithfulness lie at the heart of our hope.

Reflect…

Bring your own experience of faithfulness and unfaithfulness before God and, if necessary, ask for healing. Ask him to show you his own faithfulness to you, as if set in relief.

Faithful God, you set a rainbow in the sky, an arc of colour and light to remind me that the promise maker keeps his promises. Remind me that your promises are never empty, your faithfulness is sure, and that my hope is eternal.

HOPE EMBRACED

The parable of the lost son is one of the most powerful illustrations of our Father God's love for his wayward children. Read the whole parable in Luke 15:11–31 if you have time.

'I will set out and go back to my father and say to him: "Father, I have sinned against heaven and against you. I am no longer worthy to be called your son; make me like one of your hired men."' So he got up and went to his father. But while he was still a long way off, his father saw him and was filled with compassion for him; he ran to his son, threw his arms around him and kissed him. The son said to him, 'Father, I have sinned against heaven and against you. I am no longer worthy to be called your son.'

LUKE 15:18–21

If such a thing were possible, I would conduct a survey of everyone reading this page to discover how many of us would point to this parable as our favourite. I would hazard a guess that many of us would raise our hands. Its very essence is the wonderful truth that our heavenly Father is always on the lookout for us. Even when we feel as if we have wandered out of his care, he sees us and begins to run to us while we are still 'far off'. He welcomes us with open arms, wherever we have been and whatever we have done. So often we will wander away, in weakness or disillusion, living our own lives with our back firmly turned towards the Father who looks out for us and longs to welcome us home.

Jesus used this parable to describe perfectly the grace and forgiveness at the heart of the rescue and reconciliation package for which he would give his life. Many of us long for reconciliation.

Ernest Hemingway once wrote a short story, *The Capital of the World*, set in Spain, in which a father and son fell out and the son left home and ran away to Madrid. Years later the father thought better of his actions, realized that he might have been too harsh and resolved to find his son. He put an advert in a Madrid newspaper, which read, 'Paco, meet me at the Hotel Montana at noon on Tuesday. All is forgiven. Papa.' But Paco is a common name in Spain, and when the father arrived on Tuesday he had to force his way through a large crowd of young men, all called Paco, and all wanting to be reconciled with their fathers.[15]

There are many parents who, like Paco's father and the father in the parable, long for a wayward child to come home. Maybe you are one of them, and this Christmas has been empty without the son or daughter whose whereabouts are unclear, and whose apparent rejection of your parental love wounds you deeply. The parable of the lost (or 'prodigal') son gives hope to those waiting for their own 'prodigals', not just because it tells us that it is never too late but because we can be aware of the empathy of a Father God who longs for the return of his children—and our children—who has compassion for them and never gives up. We can know for certain that he understands the pain, the loss, the bewilderment that fill our wakeful nights and long 'I wonder where…?' days. He knows how it feels to give love to his children, only to hear them mock him, deny him and pour scorn on that love so freely given. We can be sure that he feels the icy cold of abandonment, the helplessness of letting go and the cry of forsakenness. He also knows what it is to watch and wait and look out into the darkness, waiting for the return of a son. Perhaps the most comforting words we can hear him say when our hearts are breaking for the loss of our children are 'I know, I know'—because he does.

In his book, *Bringing Home the Prodigals*[16], Rob Parsons recounts a story he heard as he began to work on the manuscript. He was staying in a guesthouse on the beautiful Gower Peninsula in Wales and, while taking a break outside and enjoying the view across the bay, was joined by a priest who was leading a retreat. He writes:

We began chatting and he asked me what I was doing. When I told him I was writing a book about prodigals he told me a most incredible story. Let me try to capture his words as I remember them:

Near here in the village of Mumbles is an old large house. An elderly lady lives there alone and every night in an attic window there is always a light on. Her son left home twenty-five years ago, rather like the prodigal in your book, but she has never given up the hope that one day he will come home. We all know the house well and often gaze up as we pass to check, but although the bulb must at times burn out we have never seen that house without a light on.

It is for her son.

Those words remind us that God will always leave a light on for us. It is a sign of our hope for reconciliation meeting his forgiveness in embrace. What is it that keeps that lamp burning? Love, and the inability to forget the one we love—a sense of the embrace of a Father God for us, and so for them. But most of all it is the indescribable, almost unspeakable essence of hope that God has placed within us.

Reflect...

When have you been aware of the Father watching out for you from 'a long way off'?

> *Welcoming Father,*
> *While I was still a long way off,*
> *you looked out for me,*
> *and therein lies my continuing hope—*
> *hope of life eternal, hope of you.*
> *Thank you for your arms outstretched,*
> *for the light that never goes out.*
> *Hold me in your embrace.*

CHRIS: THE HOMECOMING

But the father said to his servants, 'Quick, bring the best robe and put it on him. Put a ring on his finger and sandals on his feet. Bring the fattened calf and kill it. Let's have a feast and celebrate. For this son of mine was dead and is alive again; he was lost and is found.' So they began to celebrate.

LUKE15:22–24

Chris Coffey lives and works in Cardiff, Wales. He grew up in a Christian home, the eldest son of a Baptist minister. He studied English at Queen's University, Belfast, taught in South India and now works for a community arts project called The Gate. This is his homecoming story.[17]

'Now, in my mid-20s, I can say that I live for Jesus and mean it in the most definite and down-to-earth way. But it hasn't always been like that. Every journey has a story: this is mine.

'At age 5 I sat on a closed toilet seat and prayed with my dad crouching beside me. It was the only quiet place we could find to ask God to come into the life of a happy, curious, average boy with Christian parents. I remember few details except the size of the room and the fact that my feet hardly touched the wooden floors, but I remember knowing that this was a big deal. Seven years later I dropped and surfaced in a baptism pool, watching bubbles chase above me, trying to remember every moment in perfect detail for later reference. When I spoke in front of the assembled church, I declared Jesus publicly as God, as my God, and it was real.

'After that, life came at me thick and fast, fun and tempting. It became difficult to focus on a spiritual life that promised its rewards elsewhere. I was your average teenager. I was more than a little torn, pulled in two directions for years, unwilling to reject either of those two worlds—one because it was too beautiful and tragic and offered too much; the other, the one with the eternal dimension, because deep down I knew it was real.

'God had been here, walked this earth and wanted more from me—I believed that much. However, I felt no nearer to him in the corporate gatherings of his followers than I did walking the streets at night. I didn't see God in church or nature or anywhere at all. I hung in there, part of the youth group, while sermons washed over me like adverts. I saw no examples of Christians I aspired to be like, and the Bible seemed a confusing anthology of badly written morality tales. But at the hub of all this rejection, and below a thin surface of resentment, was a solid but unimpressive sense that it was all true. Even he slipped by unnoticed—the Jesus that I would later find so compelling. Now, he is my reason for forward motion; then, all I had was a two-dimensional cardboard cut-out, meek, mild and totally voiceless.

'The period in my life when I was at university was probably the furthest that I have ever been from God. I made it through most of it without giving him a second thought, but, towards the end of my time, I would find myself awake in the middle of the night or caught off guard with my thoughts straying on to big questions. Everything I saw seemed to point to him or find its way round to him in conversation. Eventually, after finishing my degree and leaving the country, I met God 6000 miles from home, in the last place I expected to find him. It turns out he likes to chase!

'Working with some very poor young people, I found myself challenged about what I valued in life. I began meeting with a small group of people who I found I could relate to, despite our different backgrounds, nationalities and types of faith, whether we were leaning over a beer or an open Bible. I found a community of people willing to listen, looking outwards and wanting to know God better today than they did yesterday. I saw church how it was intended to be—a living, serving community of Christians meeting real needs with a radical love.

'Now, I am involved with an "experimental" church in a city centre pub in my spare time. Essentially it's a church for people who don't like conventional churches, and we meet a variety of people. Some have had no previous Christian contact in their life; others have and were either mistreated or didn't "fit in". But there's another group of people who are re-testing the Christian faith, those who have heard it all before and went away, only to find that nothing else out there makes sense. They've been there, they have the T-shirt but they want something more. I have a lot of time for prodigals. I've seen what God can do when they come back. God is totally concerned with us.

'Unless you believe Jesus was exaggerating, or being over-dramatic for his audience, the parable stands as a lesson about how God waits, and the kind of party he throws when we come home.'

Reflect...

In your notebook, either write a letter to a family member or friend who is the prodigal you long to see return home, or write your own letter of confession and reconciliation to the Father, as a returning prodigal. Set your letter before God in prayer.

Father, whether I am the prodigal or whether I long for the return of a prodigal, let me witness the forgiveness and safety of your welcoming arms.

LIFELONG HOPE

But as for me, I will always have hope;
I will praise you more and more.
My mouth will tell of your righteousness,
of your salvation all day long,
though I know not its measure.
I will come and proclaim your mighty acts, O Sovereign Lord;
I will proclaim your righteousness, yours alone.
Since my youth, O God, you have taught me,
and to this day I declare your marvellous deeds.
Even when I am old and grey,
do not forsake me, O God,
till I declare your power to the next generation,
your might to all who are to come.

PSALM 71:14–18

Our hope in God is a lifelong hope, a sure and certain hope. We may, like Dawn, whose long wait for a husband we shared earlier, be asked to give up our hope in things, people, places and ambitions, temporarily or permanently, because God wants us to hope first and foremost in him. Like Chris in yesterday's reading, we may turn our back on that hope, only to find it again with renewed vigour, so that 'he is our reason for forward motion'. Very often when we look back over our lives, we may see disappointments, broken dreams, dashed hopes. But we will also see the hand of God covering our days with a canopy of stronger, more permanent hope—a hope that has shielded us through those days of loss and disappointment and will continue to cover us until it can be removed, and we can bask in the light of his glory as that true hope is fulfilled and we are in his presence.

We hope in God...

With innocence...
in the dependent days of infancy,
when time isn't known.

With simplicity...
across the skittish days of childhood,
when time doesn't matter.

With dreams...
through the bold, confident and foolish days of youth,
as time is wasted.

With confidence...
Amid the years of building—career, home, family,
as time is chased.

With trust...
As we let go, face 'empty nests', feel fragile,
and wonder if we still have time.

With frailty...
When our long-term memory is the clearest,
and time has flown far into the distance.

Into eternity...
Where at last we will know our true homecoming,
and our time will come.

Reflect...

Read Psalm 71 again. Ask yourself:

- *How can I tell of God's righteousness and mighty acts?*
- *How can I fulfil my responsibility to declare his power to the next generation?*

Look back over your life, and use your notebook to trace your hope in God. Look at the ways his hand has been on your life. You may find it helpful to draw a timeline, beginning with your birth or babyhood, moving to this moment and beyond. Place the major events and clear memories of God's leading and presence above and below the line, top and bottom—top for 'high' points, bottom for 'low' times.

- *Where has the hope of God sustained you most?*
- *How do your discoveries build your confidence for the future?*

God of eternity,
my hope has been in you,
through the shifting sands of time,
in the moments of quiet joy,
the pacing hours of pain,
past long days of disappointment,
in the weary weeks of waiting,
across the years of fading dreams.
Remind me that though small hopes are dashed,
opportunities have been missed,
dreams have turned to nightmares,
longings are unanswered
and old regrets still sting,
my hope in you is certain.
My wait is not in vain.

✢

WHEN THE WAITING IS OVER

GALLERY: 'THE ARRIVAL'

Here, finally, is the twin—the second painting that links to the very first canvas you looked at. It is the painting you have been glimpsing in the far distance as you have stepped through each interconnecting room of this extraordinary gallery. It is the largest, most prominent work on display. The same vibrant colours are used here as in the first painting. They are added with the same detail and vitality of style. But here the colours are almost impossibly brighter, illuminated not so much by the spotlight above but by the golden glow the artist has painted above and beyond the crowd. It has a luminescent quality you have never seen before. You would love to examine it more closely, but the canvas is so large that the upper part of the painting is out of reach. You can focus on the lower half, though, where the colours are still intense and jewel-like. Here are ruby reds and violet mauves, every shade of pink and purple, jade green and turquoise, deep butter yellow and inky blue. It is a brilliant array of every colour in the spectrum, like a stained-glass window, seemingly lit from beyond and behind.

Now you look closely at the detail. Again the artist has depicted a crowd. At first you think this must be a different gathering from the first, such is the contrast in facial expression, colour and demeanour, but looking closer you recognize one or two faces—faces that appeared not just in the first painting of the pair, but in subsequent works throughout the gallery.

The woman who at first stood alone, weeping, even when surrounded by a crowd, is no longer weeping. She is surrounded by others, almost leaping, her face uplifted, her tears vanished. And here is the cook who, in the first painting, had been busily tasting the mixture in his bowl. Now he proudly carries his finished cake, gleaming with sugar frosting and prepared for a party. Laughing children follow in his path, eager for a taste.

To one side, jazz musicians play together, a hundred different instruments raised to the sky in a blast of glorious, jubilant noise. They seem to be leading what you now realize is a procession—a carnival, perhaps. It is certainly a celebration.

Near the top of the painting you notice a particularly finely dressed man. A nobleman or prince, perhaps? He is part of the leading crowd. To your amazement, you realize that this is the beggar who had held out his hand in need in that first painting. Now his rags have been swapped for finery. His scar, once so disfiguring, is still visible but has faded and now only adds to the character and beauty of his face. He is walking boldly beside the blind man, whose arm is raised, his finger pointing with certainty, his eyes fixed ahead with clear sight into the distance.

Groups of friends in threes, fours and fives walk together, arms linked. Others run towards each other in recognition or are painted lost in the warm embrace of greeting or exchanging the handshake of reunion. These are the characters who were earlier set in the stone of sculpture, miraculously brought to life.

Here are the trapeze artists, their garments gleaming in the light, not a speck of sawdust on their feet, no marks from the highwire on their shoes, arms entwined as if they are about to bow to an invisible audience. And here is the woman in the shawl, no longer looking out to sea but reunited with her fisherman husband, their child held between them. There is no anxiety in her expression, no stormy emotion in her eyes. Her hope has been fulfilled.

You see renewal of life and vigour here. The feet of the old no longer falter; neither are youths held up in frustration or infants lost, bewildered, in the crowd.

Near the top of the painting you see the clock, that magnificent timepiece you studied so closely earlier. It seems smaller now, tucked under the arm of a tall figure in white who is striding at the head of the procession. Both the hands of the clock hang limp, without tension or precision. The door of the case has fallen open. You cannot see closely from this distance, but you feel sure that the little character that ran so aimlessly within its case will have reached his destination, stopped his hurrying and put away his pocket watch. Despite the clock's fine craftsmanship and rich history, the tall figure pays it little attention as he walks, as if it has fulfilled its role and is now redundant.

Lifting your gaze a little higher, you notice that the crowd is entering gates that are swung wide and hung with 'welcome' banners and rich decoration. This is the end of their journey. This is arrival. The waiting is over.

If only you could take a glimpse beyond those gates, follow the crowd in celebration, be part of the scene that awaits them. But for now, at least, it is beyond your gaze. You will have to wait...

INTRODUCTION

We've discovered that God asks us to wait throughout our spiritual lives and that, if we are to become accomplished in the art of waiting, we must learn the skills and develop a sense of God's own perspective. We must learn from those who have gone before, and from each other. We must develop patience and attend to the groundwork of faith, seek to build community among our fellow 'artists', and take time out to be with the Master, never losing hope that one day our waiting will be over and we will see his final masterpiece—a masterpiece temporarily hidden, but one day to be enjoyed by all who have learnt the art of waiting.

In these last two days of reading and meditation, we will take some time to reflect on the fulfilment of that eternal hope. We shall reward ourselves with a peep at what lies hidden at the end of our wait, and discover how we can be sure of receiving what we are waiting for—eternal life in the presence of our God.

FACE TO FACE

Today's two Bible passages finally begin to colour in the pencil outlines that we drew right at the very beginning of Advent. They give us a tantalizing glimpse of what lies ahead of us, of what we have been promised—everything that makes the waiting worthwhile.

Dear friends, now we are children of God, and what we will be has not yet been made known. But we know that when he appears, we shall be like him, for we shall see him as he is.

1 JOHN 3:2

One of the hardest things about the Christian life, at least for me, is not being able to see Jesus. I just long to see him! It's tough loving someone when you can't see them, never have seen them, and only have a few clues to what standing face to face with them will be like. It must be a bit like falling in love with a penfriend. You write wonderful newsy letters for months, even years, talk on the phone often, write long e-mails in the middle of the night, resist the temptation to send each other photos; and then you unexpectedly find yourself not only in their country but also in their home town. It's the moment you've been waiting for. At last you can see what he or she is really like. It could turn out to be a delightful surprise or it could be a terrible shock!

One of my favourite films is *You've Got Mail*. Kathleen (Meg Ryan) and Joe (Tom Hanks) conduct a wonderful anonymous e-mail friendship, charming each other with beautifully written vignettes, and sharing their deepest thoughts and reflections on life, without revealing their true identity. While Kathleen runs a small children's bookshop, Joe is the head of a huge chain of bookstores—Fox Books. When a new Fox Books superstore opens in her neighbourhood, Kathleen is gradually forced out of business by the new store and grows to loathe the Joe she meets in this context, still unaware that he is also her 'Mr E-mail' friend.

Their e-mail friendship continues unaware and unharmed, and eventually they decide to meet. On the way to the meeting, Joe discovers that his e-mail friend and Kathleen are one and the same. He is shocked at first, but as he admits his true feelings for her, at least to himself, he realizes that she must get to know him—and love him—as he really is. Knowing that she will run a mile if she discovers who he is before that happens, he sets out to ask her forgiveness, gain her trust and woo her as the big bookstore owner he really is.

As the two fall in love, neither admitting it to each other, we have the sneaking suspicion that Kathleen is becoming increasingly aware of who Joe might be. Far from running a mile, she begins to hope beyond hope that Joe and Mr E-mail are the very same. On the day she has arranged to meet Mr E-Mail, Joe (as Fox Books) shares his feelings with Kathleen, but they part awkwardly, still not fully able to see each other as they really are, face to face. Of course, there has to be a happy ending, so when Kathleen goes to meet Mr E-mail, she is not disappointed. As she jumps up and down, trying to see him coming around the corner, it is, of course, Joe who appears. As she falls into his arms she says, 'I wanted it to be you, I wanted it to be you so much!' (And we all go 'Aaaahhh!')

When we finally meet Jesus, it will be a million times better than that. We will know the excitement of having found the one we have talked to, listened to, loved and longed for. I get so excited at the thought of that moment. How will I control myself? Will I be leaping up and down trying to catch a glimpse of him before he appears, or will I suddenly find myself face to face with him and just know—'It's you!'? Of course we can't know for sure, but we do know, from Paul's words, that we shall be like him and will see him face to face as he is (1 John 3:2; 1 Corinthians 13:12).

Won't it be great just to be able to gaze at him? To catch the expression in his eyes, the amusement in the curl of his mouth? To be able to speak to him face to face and hear his answer, his laughter on the wind? I can't wait! But of course, I have to. It's what this whole book has been about.

What a thing to be waiting for—Jesus himself! And what's more, we'll live with him for ever.

Then I saw a new heaven and a new earth, for the first heaven and the first earth had passed away, and there was no longer any sea. I saw the Holy City, the new Jerusalem, coming down out of heaven from God, prepared as a bride beautifully dressed for her husband. And I heard a loud voice from the throne saying, 'Now the dwelling of God is with men, and he will live with them. They will be his people, and he will live with them. They will be his people, and God himself will be with them and be their God. He will wipe every tear from their eyes. There will be no more death or mourning or crying or pain, for the old order of things has passed away.'

He who was seated on the throne said, 'I am making everything new!' Then he said, 'Write this down, for these words are trustworthy and true.'

REVELATION 21:1–5

Every so often a news programme will include a report of a visit by the Queen to a very ordinary household in a very ordinary area. She will be seen driving through a housing estate in her shiny black car, and we will watch intrigued as she is welcomed into a very ordinary three-bedroom semi by, let's say, a Mrs Watson and her family. Mrs Watson will pour tea and hand the Queen a chocolate digestive or two, carefully arranged on a plate, which the Queen will graciously decline. Both will behave as if this kind of thing happens every day. Yet we all know that Mrs Watson, her sister Jean, her mum and three neighbours have spent the day dusting and polishing—and, of course, cleaning the loo, just in case it should be needed! There is a lace tablecloth borrowed from a friend and cups and saucers bought specially, and when the Queen has left, Mrs Watson will be the most popular and talked-about person in the town for a day or two—just because the Queen came to tea. Her family will never be allowed to use 'those' cups and saucers, and the friend will frame the lace tablecloth and display it in her dining-room above a small homemade plaque.

Yet we are going to live with the king of heaven and earth—and he will live with us! No brief visit and polite chit-chat: he is going to dwell with us for ever. Such knowledge reminds me that God was so close to Adam and Eve that he was heard 'walking in the garden in the cool of the day' (Genesis 3:8), and yet they lost that privilege. Because of his grace and love for us, however, he will once more walk with us, talk with us and live with us. The story will come full circle; the picture will be complete. The masterpiece will receive its finishing touches. We will receive what we have been waiting for, because God keeps his promises.

Reflect...

Spend time visualizing the end of our waiting time, when we will see Jesus.

O God of promises, as you prepare a place for me with you, help me keep a place for you in my life, in my heart, in my mind. As you do not forget me, don't let me forget you.

AT LAST...

When God made his promise to Abraham, since there was no one greater for him to swear by, he swore by himself, saying, 'I will surely bless you and give you many descendants.' And so after waiting patiently, Abraham received what was promised. Men swear by someone greater than themselves, and the oath confirms what is said and puts an end to all argument. Because God wanted to make the unchanging nature of his purpose very clear to the heirs of what was promised, he confirmed it with an oath. God did this so that, by two unchangeable things in which it is impossible for God to lie, we who have fled to take hold of the hope offered to us may be greatly encouraged. We have this hope as an anchor for the soul, firm and secure. It enters the inner sanctuary behind the curtain, where Jesus, who went before us, has entered on our behalf. He has become a high priest for ever, in the order of Melchizedek.

HEBREWS 6:13–20

We live close to the sea, in a coastal city with more marinas, yacht clubs and boatyards than parks. In the summer we are sometimes held up when driving into town, finding ourselves crawling along in the car behind a vast carrier taking a huge yacht or cruiser to its moorings. When these magnificent craft have been prepared for the water, they are lined up alongside the pontoons, awaiting their crew or the weekend sailing enthusiasts and millionaires who will spend time on them. Some of the larger craft may be taken to sea only a handful of times through the season, and in between times will remain moored and bobbing gently in the water alongside a host of gleaming white companions. They may wait days, or even weeks, before being taken out into the waters of Plymouth Sound where they can really come into their own.

Smaller craft are often motored out to drop anchor further up river, where their owners can find slightly cheaper moorings, because of the inconvenience of shuttling to and fro in a dinghy to get on board. The security of these craft depends on their firm anchor, without which they would be tossed around in the first storm to hit, or drift aimlessly before running aground.

The writer of Hebrews tells us that, in taking hold of the eternal hope given to us by God, we are securing a firm anchor for our souls—an anchor that will hold us firm and secure, however long we have to wait, however disappointed we might become and whatever the weather through which we have to wait. Our anchor of hope will hold us secure in a safe harbour or in the midst of a storm.

Right at the beginning of our Advent readings, we reflected on Abraham's lifetime of waiting, reminding ourselves that while he never saw the fulfilment of God's promise that he would become a great nation, he never gave up hope. He may have been discouraged, wondered 'How long, O Lord?' or even felt tempted to give up altogether, but he believed God. 'So after waiting patiently, Abraham received what was promised' (Hebrews 6:15). Abraham's promise is ours too.

I don't know whether you picked up this book because it was about waiting and you are finding that act difficult right now, or whether you chose it specifically because it was an Advent book. Either way, I hope that you have discovered (or, like me, rediscovered) through these daily reflections that God does use our waiting in a creative and exciting way, however we might feel at the time.

Through our waiting…

- He teaches us to trust and to live in obedience.
- He builds our faith.
- He develops our patience.

- He draws us into community.
- He gives us opportunities to share his love with others.
- He reveals more of himself.
- He teaches us to pray.
- He nurtures our relationship with him.
- He gives us hope.
- He turns our eyes towards what we are ultimately waiting for... himself.

Reflect...

Take some time now to look back through your notes, prayers and comments from the last month or so.

What has God taught you in each of the areas above? What has he said to you in the quietness of your heart?

How might you take the lessons learnt from waiting into the new year?

Father, as we wait for your purposes to be fulfilled, give us patience, teach us to trust, and fill us with hope, reminding us that we do not wait in vain.

AFTERWORD

Like Abraham, after waiting patiently, we too will receive what God has promised.

He who testifies to these things says, 'Yes, I am coming soon.' Amen. Come, Lord Jesus. The grace of the Lord Jesus be with God's people. Amen.

REVELATION 22:20–21

notes

1 David Stewart-David, Lecturer in Logistics and Transport, University of Northumberland, *BBC News Online*, 6 October 2000.

2 Josh McDowell, *Evidence that Demands a Verdict*, Campus Crusade for Christ, 1972.

3 Robert Cowley, *What If?*, Pan, 1999.

4 Hilary McDowell, *Some Day I'm Going to Fly*, Triangle, 1995, p. 3.

5 Adapted from Laurie Lee, *Cider with Rosie*, Penguin, 1955.

6 Report by Richard Johnson in the *Sunday Times Magazine*, February 2003.

7 Debra's story can be read in Debra Veal, *Rowing it Alone*, Robson Books, 2002.

8 This prayer was written for the Care for the Family Christmas appeal 2001. Used with permission.

9 James Jones, *People of the Blessing*, BRF, 1998.

10 Joni Eareckson Tada and Steve Estes, *When God Weeps*, Zondervan, 1997, p. 124.

11 Laurence Singlehurst, *Beyond the Clouds*, Hodder & Stoughton, 2002, p. 66.

12 Jenny Francis, *Belief Beyond Pain*, SPCK, 1992, quoted in Julie Sheldon, *One Step at a Time*, Hodder & Stoughton, 2000, p. 153.

13 Figures from *Moving Forward Together*, Lord Chancellor's Department, 2002.

14 Robert Frost, *Selected Poems*, ed. Ian Hamilton, Penguin, 1969, p. 130.

15 Adapted from Philip Yancey, *True Confessions*, Word, 1987, pp. 42–43.

16 Rob Parsons, *Bringing Home the Prodigals*, Hodder & Stoughton, 2002. Used with permission of the publishers.

17 Chris's story originally appeared in Rob Parsons, *Bringing Home the Prodigals* and has been adapted here for inclusion with permission.

also By wendy Bray

wInner: BIogRaphy of the year,
chrIstIan Book awaRds 2002

IN THE PALM OF
GOD'S HAND

A DIARY OF LIVING AGAINST THE ODDS

'Sharing a diary like this is about more than baring your soul. It's like taking your clothes off in public in mid-January and asking passers-by to throw snowballs at you. Not something you would do unless you hoped an awful lot of good would come of it. But here I am, doing it... Whatever good might result is God's to reveal. I would hope that it will involve glory to him and comfort and encouragement to others, as well as providing the occasional laugh.'

This prayer diary testifies how personal faith can transform the hardest of times, and how God's love nd mercy still break through, no matter how tough the situation. Rob Parsons writes in the introduction: 'This is a book about trust. Not the kind of trust that says, "I know that soon it will be all right again", but rather the kind that trusts God—anyway—sometimes because there is just nowhere else to go.'

ISBN 1 84101 336 6   £6.99

Available from your local Christian bookshop or direct from BRF using the order form on page 191.

also from BRF

BRF's Lent Book 2005

CHALLENGES OF THE NARROW WAY

Bridget Plass

'Enter through the narrow gate; for the gate is wide and the road is easy that leads to destruction, and there are many who take it. For the gate is narrow and the road is hard that leads to life, and there are few who find it' (Matthew 7:13–14). These words of Jesus challenge all who want to follow his way, choosing the path that leads to eternal life.

In *Challenges of the Narrow Way*, Bridget Plass has written a book for Lent that encourages us to face up to the fact that God's calling may not be to a comfortable, successful life, with all emotional and material needs fulfilled. Instead, he calls us simply to follow, taking us on a journey that may be hard, lonely and at times dangerous, but one that leads ultimately to 'treasure in heaven'. And if we acknowledge our weakness, our fear and our sense of unworthiness, he will give us sufficient strength to carry on, every step of the way.

ISBN 1 84101 365 X   £7.99

Available from your local Christian bookshop or direct from BRF using the order form on page 191.

A HEART TO LISTEN

BECOMING A LISTENING PERSON IN A NOISY WORLD

Michael Mitton

Listening has become a lost art in a world that is growing ever noisier, more superficial and more stressed. Too many of us have forgotten not only about listening to others but also about listening to God, to our own hearts, to our wider communities—and even to our planet. Without listening, how can we hope to gain wisdom, to build deep and truly caring relationships with all kinds of people, to share our faith?

This accessible book shows how, with God's help, we can relearn the art of listening and in doing so become a source of help and healing for others and for ourselves. Biblical reflection is interwoven with insights from the author's wide experience of listening ministry in the UK and abroad. Between each chapter are episodes of an intriguing story, which explores the book's themes through vividly imagined characters in a cross-cultrual setting.

ISBN 1 84101 269 6   £7.99

Available from your local Christian bookshop or direct from BRF using the order form on page 191.

ORDER FORM

REF	TITLE	PRICE	QTY	TOTAL
336 6	*In the Palm of God's Hand*	£6.99		
365 X	*Challenges of the Narrow Way*	£7.99		
269 6	*A Heart to Listen*	£7.99		

POSTAGE AND PACKING CHARGES					Postage and packing:	
order value	UK	Europe	Surface	Air Mail	Donation:	
£7.00 & under	£1.25	£3.00	£3.50	£5.50	**Total enclosed:**	
£7.01–£30.00	£2.25	£5.50	£6.50	£10.00		
Over £30.00	free	prices on request				

Name _____ Account Number _____

Address _____

_____ Postcode _____

Telephone Number _____ Email _____

Payment by: Cheque ❑ Mastercard ❑ Visa ❑ Postal Order ❑ Switch ❑

Credit card no. ❑❑❑❑ ❑❑❑❑ ❑❑❑❑ ❑❑❑❑ Expires ❑❑ ❑❑

Switch card no. ❑❑❑❑❑❑❑❑❑❑❑❑❑❑❑❑❑❑❑❑

Issue no. of Switch card ❑❑❑❑ Expires ❑❑ ❑❑

Signature _____ Date _____

All orders must be accompanied by the appropriate payment.

Please send your completed order form to:
BRF, First Floor, Elsfield Hall, 15–17 Elsfield Way, Oxford OX2 8FG
Tel. 01865 319700 / Fax. 01865 319701 Email: enquiries@brf.org.uk

❑ Please send me further information about BRF publications.

Available from your local Christian bookshop. **BRF is a Registered Charity**

Resourcing your spiritual journey

through...

- Bible reading notes
- Books for Advent & Lent
- Books for Bible study and prayer
- Books to resource those working with under 11s in school, church and at home

- Quiet days and retreats
- Training for primary teachers and children's leaders
- Godly Play
- Barnabas Live

For more information, visit the **brf** website at **www.brf.org.uk**